All About Poetry

Co Antrim & Co Londonderry

Edited by Donna Samworth

This book belongs to

First published in Great Britain in 2010 by

Remus House
Coltsfoot Drive
Peterborough
PE2 9JX
Telephone: 01733 890066
Website: www.youngwriters.co.uk

All Rights Reserved
Book Design by Spencer Hart
© Copyright Contributors 2010
SB ISBN 978-1-84924-974-4

Foreword

At Young Writers our defining aim is to promote an enjoyment of reading and writing amongst children and young adults. By giving aspiring poets the opportunity to see their work in print, their love of the written word as well as confidence in their own abilities have the chance to blossom.

Our latest competition *Poetry Express* was designed to introduce primary school children to the wonders of creative expression. They were given free reign to write on any theme and in any style, thus encouraging them to use and explore a variety of different poetic forms.

We are proud to present the resulting collection of regional anthologies which are an excellent showcase of young writing talent. With such a diverse range of entries received, the selection process was difficult yet very rewarding.

From comical rhymes to poignant verses, there is plenty to entertain and inspire within these pages. We hope you agree that this collection bursting with imagination is one to treasure.

Contents

Broughshane Primary School, Ballymena
Philip Gregg (11) 1
Susannah Graham (10) 2
Matthew Haridy (7) 2
Cameron McNeill (11) 3
Chloe Montgomery (8) 3
Lynne Murray (11) 4
Hannah Kennedy (8) 4
Holly Harkness (11) 5
Craig Francey (7) 5
Jonathan Loughridge (11) 6
Peter McCormill (8) 6
Lewis Church (10) 7
Lee McAllister 7
Joey Lee (10) 8
Naomi Crawford (10) 8
Kathleen Witherspoon (11) 9
Robert Gordon (9) 9
Emma-Lee Wray (11) 10
Josh Houston (10) 10
Caitlin Lennon (11) 11
David Hamilton (9) 11
Thomas Ferguson (11) 12
Jodie Hanna (8) 12
Emma Purdy (11) 13
Emma Catherine Speirs (9) 13
Erin Douglas (9) 14
Daniel Lynn (9) 14
Caitlin Caldwell (11) 15
Rhys Frew (9) 15
Rebecca Marcus (10) 16
Amy Stirling (9) 16
Daniel Thomas McCalmont (9) 17
Kirill Sakharov (8) 17
Rachel Fleming (9) 18
Lucy McCormill (9) 18
Lois Smyrell (8) 19
David Stevenson (10) 19
Lucinda Wiley (10) 20
Andrew McKee (10) 20
Grace McNeill (10) 21

Shane Gibson (11) 21
Jamie Wray (9) 22
Jessica O'Neill (9) 22
Shannon Gillan (7) 22
Chloé Alexandra Leitch (9) 23
Naomi Lamont (9) 23
Lewis McDowell (8) 24
Lauren Burrows (10) 24
Lucy Millar (8) 24
Kirsty McKillop (10) 25
Emma Hamilton (9) 25
Faith Lamont (8) 25
Adele Herron (8) 26
Nicola Kernohan (9) 26
Alastair McKee (8) 26
Ben Armstrong (8) 27
Courtney Walsh (10) 27
Megan Wilmot (7) 27
Sophie Dennison (9) 28
Chloe Church (8) 28
Niall Douglas (7) 28
Scott Francey (9) 29
Ellen Moffett (8) 29
Connor McNeill (8) 29
Mark Thompson (10) 30
Jamie Houston (9) 30
Heather Balmer (8) 30
Laura Craig (9) 31
Courtney Lewis (10) 31
Rebeka Church (8) 31
Oscar Robinson (8) 32
Kate Hamilton (7) 32
Josh Balmer (8) 32
Lydia McMullan (8) 33
Alyssa Alexander (9) 33
Lucy Gibson (7) 33
James Gordon (7) 34
Stuart McNeill (8) 34
Sam Frew (8) 34
Leah Gillan (7) 35
Matthew Bruce Grimsley (7) 35
Robert Boyd (7) 35

Jamie Alexander (8) 36
Amy Murray (8) 36
Robert O'Neill (7) 36
Timothy Brown (7) 37
Jamie Knox (7) 37
Rachel Greer (8) 37
Laura Kernohan (7) 38
Jake Nicoletti (8) 38
Ben Purdy (7) 38

**Culmore Primary School,
Londonderry**
Jamie Cooke (11) 39
Caitlin Greene (11) 39
Ronan Timlin (10) 40
Mark Bell (9) 40
Ava Wilson (10) 41
Conal Gilliland (11) 41
Mathew Agavriloaie (8) 42
Emerald Jane Hockley (10) 42
Eorann Ryan Griffin (8) 42
Cara Gilliland (8) 43
Jack Twells (9) 43
Orrian Quigley (9) 43
Niamh Doherty (7) 44
Abbey Kinsella (9) 44
Jarvis Bell (7) 44
Tommy Orr (8) 45
Chiara Fiorentini (8) 45

**Donegall Road Primary School,
Belfast**
Courtney Annett (10) 45
Darrel Williams (10) 46
Carl McGrath (10) 46
Corin Henry (10) 46
Rebecca Harrison (10) 47
Alannah Gilliland (9) 47

**Eden Primary School,
Carrickfergus**
Leah Barrons (10) 47
Rachel Moore (10) 48
Louise Shields (10) 48
Heather Briers (10) 49
Demi-Louise Harper (9) 49
Anna Coulter (9) 50
Victoria Phillips (10) 50
Joel Colligan (10) 51

Sam Lilburn (10) 51
Scott Nichol (10) 51
Emily Jane Iles (10) 52
Rebecca Reid (10) 52
Nathan Christopher Adams (10) 53
Corey Steele (9) 53
Kristen Kavanagh (10) 53
Joshua Lee Johnston (9) 54
David Seaman (10) 54
Katie Louise Patterson (9) 54

**Irish Society's Primary School,
Coleraine**
Peter Forde (11) 55
Natasha Brownlee (11) 56
Grace Rosborough (11) 57
Rosanna Aimee Johnston (10) 58
Kent Morton (10) 58
Brett Wade (11) 59
Aaron Millar (10) 59
Amy Allen (10) 60
Ethan Kelly (10) 60
Victoria Lynch (11) 61
Saima Asghar (10) 61
Anna McKeown (10) 62
Olivia Marshall (10) 62
Amy Claire Cutler (11) 63
Ben Clarke (10) 63
Olivia Walker (11) 64
Sarah Harte (10) 64
Oliver Warke (11) 65
Chelsea Irwin (11) 65
Emma Louise Bell (10) 66
Chloe Rae (11) 66
Niamh McMullan (10) 67
Michael Diamond (11) 67
Lewis Mitchell (11) 68
Demi-Lee Friel (11) 68
Emma Tran (11) 69
Danielle Mullan (10) 69
Paulina Marszalek (10) 70
Macauley Whitehead (11) 70
Sara Carr (10) 71
James Hancock (10) 71
Ryan Jamison (11) 72
Alexandra O'Neill (11) 72
Alyx Campbell (10) 72
Sydney Rosier (10) 73

Cavan Tayler (11) 73
Robyn McCracken (11) 73

Kilmoyle Primary School, Ballymoney
Hannah McCurdy (11) 74
Tori Ann Hartin (10) 75
Ashley McBride (9) 76
Verity Alicia Wilson (8) 77
Tom Hayes (10) 78
Chloé Gardiner (11) 78
Annie McIlhatton (10) 79
Sarah Bleakly (9) 80
Emma Creelman (10) 81
Abby-Jo Johnston (10) 82
Bailey Dobbin (9) 83
Sam Dowey (9) 83
Matthew Irons (10) 84
Jacob Creelman (8) 85
Sophie Howard (9) 86
Joanna Christie (9) 87
Craig Freeman (8) 88
Matthew McClean (8) 89
Johnathan Smith (9) 90
Lynzi Stirling (9) 91
Coran Martin McCook (9) 92
Victoria McKeeman (8) 93
Lyle Kennedy (9) 94
Travis Kane (10) 95
Jack Dowey (11) 95
Lois Carson (9) 96
Ellie McAlister (8) 96
Molly Elder (10) 97
Timothy Keys (10) 97
Adam McFaull (10) 98
Melissa Kane (10) 98
Charis Nevin (9) 99
Olivia Boyd (10) 99
Thomas McCrory (9) 100
Craig McKeeman (10) 100

Loanends Primary School, Crumlin
Joshua-James McKee (11) 101
William Adair (11) 101
PJ Bowman (11) 101
Joshua Walker (11) 102
Sophie Martin (11) 102

Emma McWhirter (11) 102
Edward Stirling (11) 103
Philip White (11) 103
Olivia Catherine Anna Fleming (11) ... 103
Rose Marquess (11) 104

Macosquin Primary School, Coleraine
Emma Wallace (9) 104
Maxine Smyth (9) 105
Heléna Scott (9) 106
Timothy Reid (8) 107
Ben Ross (8) 108
Kaitlin Campbell (9) 109
Charlotte Dorrans (9) 110
Natasha Hall (9) 111
Marla Stewart (9) 112

St Columbas Primary School, Coleraine
Ruairí McKillop (9) 112
Dylan Mullan (10) 113
Aidan Davidson (8) 113
Megan McGilligan (7) 114
Anthony Davidson (8) 114
Grace Mullan (8) 115
Keeley Shaye Faulkner (8) 115
Mairead Tully (10) 116
Caitlín Moore (7) 116
Aoife Gallagher (8) 117
Seán McKillop (8) 117
Matthew Connolly (9) 117
Tiernán O'Connell (10) 118
Killian Mullan (9) 118
Kathleen Cassidy (9) 118
Shauna Deighan (9) 119
Jack Robinson (9) 119
Nadine O'Kane (9) 119
Hannah Mullan (9) 120

St MacNissius Primary School, Tannaghmore
Nathan James Totten (7) 120
Kimberley McCallum (7) 120
Tara Heffron (8) 121

St Paul's Primary School, Galliagh
Amy Whoriskey (10) 121
Sean Damien Reid (11) 122

Michael Anthony Lindsay (11) 123
Bradley Belgrave (10) 124
Ciara O'Doherty (10) 125
Shanice Boyle (10) 125
Christopher McQuaid (10) 126
Jack Gillen (10) 126
Aoife Robinson (10) 127
Caitlin Goodfellow (10) 127
Reece Ogle (11) 128
Rhys Dunne (10) 128
Inaam Abdallah (10) 129
Reece Moore (10) 129

Sacred Heart Primary School, Waterside
Rebecca McDermott (10) 130
Niamh Kelly (10) 131
Ben McLaughlin (10) 132
Ben Radcliff (9) 133
Shannon McConomy (9) 134
Aoifen McBrearty (10) 135
Cahir Henderson (9) 136
Aoife Strawbridge (10) 137
Sarah Owens (9) 138
Alisha Villa (10) 138
Adam McGlinchey (10) 139
Caoimhín Ballard (10) 139
Gemma Boyle (9) 140
Georgia Hildreth (9) 140

Tonagh Primary School, Lisburn
Ren Thompson (8) 141
Claire Smylie (10) 141
Lucas Jack Fitzsimmons (10) 142
Nathan Brennan (9) 142
Skye McMichael (10) 143
Dean McCann (8) 143
Ben Lancaster (8) 143
Ethan Louden (8) 144
Sarah O'Flaherty (8) 144
Katie Chesney (7) 144
Joshua Robertson (8) 145
Scott McBride 145
Skye Elizabeth Dodd (8) 145

The Poems

Skipping Game For The 21st+ Century

Geothermal energy
Good, good, good
Biodegradable
You know you should.

Recycle paper
Save that tree
Use the sun
Because it's energy.

Dont waste oil
It won't last
At the minute
It's running out fast.

Organic potatoes
They're the best
My mum says they'll put
Hairs on my chest.

Nice clean air
Yes, yes, yes
Kids of the future
They're the best.

Environment
That is good
Children of the world
Doing what they should.

Philip Gregg (11)
Broughshane Primary School, Ballymena

My Ponies

I have a pony, her name is Lilly
She is white, cute and loveable
She's my favourite pony
Because she's the sweet-tempered one
She's the one that I hunt on

I have a pony called Polly
She is tall, babyish and sweet
She's my jumping pony
She likes to jump really high
She's the one that I do cross-country on

I have a pony called Chico
He is sweet, cute and old
He's the oldest of them all
He's 30 years old
And on his way out
He's the one that I practised hunting on

I had a pony called Macora
He was really bad
I must have fallen off him twenty times
I changed his name to Teddy
And that he was not
He broke his leg and that was the end of him.
It was six days before my birthday.

Susannah Graham (10)
Broughshane Primary School, Ballymena

Bats

Are scary
Flying at you
Screeching loudly at you
Boo!

Matthew Haridy (7)
Broughshane Primary School, Ballymena

My Many Goldfish

I had a lot of goldfish
The key word in that is had.
They all died so quickly,
It was really sad.

I don't know how it happened,
What made it be?
Why does every goldfish,
Go and die on me?

There was Fergie, Goldie,
There was Becks as well.
Though when they all died,
No one could bear the smell.

We got them really cheap,
But within days they were dead.
We buried them in the backyard,
In a matchbox as their bed.

I think that there was too much noise,
Their little bodies couldn't cope.
I wish that we could get some more,
They will have a lot more hope.

Cameron McNeill (11)
Broughshane Primary School, Ballymena

If I Knew How To Fly . . .

If I knew how to fly . . .
I'd fly to sunny Spain
I'd surprise my aunty Janine
I'd fly to see JLS perform
I'd be the first to get to school
I'd have the time of my life!

Chloe Montgomery (8)
Broughshane Primary School, Ballymena

Eco-Friendly Skipping Rhyme

Eco-friendly,
Being green.
Pollution,
Is what we've seen!

Wind turbines,
Waterwheels,
Help the Earth,
That's how it feels!

Air pollution,
Cru-el-ty
Don't put waste
In the sea!

Littered streets,
An emp-ty bin,
A dirty world,
It's such a sin!

Our world could die,
But let's not see,
Let's turn it round
For you and me!

Lynne Murray (11)
Broughshane Primary School, Ballymena

If I Were Invisible . . .

If I were invisible . . .
I'd go to Spain with my sister
I'd invite my friends over . . .
Mum would never know!
I'd get no homework for the day
I'd have a super time!

Hannah Kennedy (8)
Broughshane Primary School, Ballymena

A Skipping Poem For 2010

Water, water
you must not waste
when you go to
wash your face

Wherever you are
any place
you must remember
not to waste

The sun is great
for the Earth and me
it helps us grow
the great oak tree

The waves rush in
and are trapped at the shore
and you know what?
We can keep using more

Recycled paper
save the tree
what's it all about?
Energy!

Holly Harkness (11)
Broughshane Primary School, Ballymena

If I Had A Million Pounds . . .

If I had a million pounds . . .
I'd buy tickets for a match
I'd buy a mini sports car
I'd buy a servant for *me!*
I'd help the people in Haiti
I'd have the time of my life!

Craig Francey (7)
Broughshane Primary School, Ballymena

Skipping Game For 2010

Cut the smoke
Or we'll choke.

Don't be a cheater
Turn off the heater.

Don't be a fool
Wear the wool.

No more oil
Coal, or gas.

Don't chop the trees
We need to breathe.

Geothermal
Is the best.

Ge-ner-ate
Your electricity.

Wind, sun and water,
Renewable energy.

Jonathan Loughridge (11)
Broughshane Primary School, Ballymena

If I Had A Million Pounds . . .

If I had a million pounds . . .
I'd watch Lady GaGa perform
I'd treat myself to a limo
I'd rule the world!
I'd fly to New York - *wow!*
I'd live in a posh palace
I'd be a VIP!
I'd party every night
I'd enjoy every moment!

Peter McCormill (8)
Broughshane Primary School, Ballymena

Nightmare

Once I had a nightmare,
It was really, really scary.
I was in my bed,
I heard something in my wardrobe.
Didn't know what it was
So I shouted for my mum to come.
I don't know if she heard or not
But she definitely did not come.
So I went over to the wardrobe
And opened it up wide.
Then I saw this weird crocodile-guy
And he scared me out of my wits!
So then I ran downstairs
And hid in the living room.
The crocodile-guy came after me
Then he opened the door.
So I woke up,
Nightmare over.

Lewis Church (10)
Broughshane Primary School, Ballymena

Snow

Snow is so crispy,
So white as well,
Children building snowmen,
So big and cuddly,
Everyone having snowball fights,
Getting smacked on the face so hard,
Rolling down snow,
Getting so wet,
Everyone's having fun,
Enjoying the snow as much as I do.

Lee McAllister
Broughshane Primary School, Ballymena

Eco-Friendly Skipping Rhyme

Eco-friendly
1, 2, 3
Don't chop the tree
And we'll be free

Don't trust the factories
They give smoke
So they will
Make us choke

Recycled paper
Save the trees
Use the sun
It is free

Biodegradable
1, 2, 3
Please don't put waste
In the sea.

Joey Lee (10)
Broughshane Primary School, Ballymena

The Witch

We hear a cackle
We hear the sound
Someone's creeping about
The quiet whisper of the trees
In a very cold breeze
We hear a mew
We hear a swoop
Nearer and nearer
Until it hits the window
Then the noise stops
Everything seems calm again.

Naomi Crawford (10)
Broughshane Primary School, Ballymena

Skipping Game For 2010

Chemical-free
The air should be.
The streets should be clean
A prettier scene.

Cleaner sand
On the land.
We must see
A sparkling sea.

Cut the smoke
Or we will choke.
It's in the air
Everywhere.

An organic farm
Does no harm.
Keep the trees
So we can breathe.

Kathleen Witherspoon (11)
Broughshane Primary School, Ballymena

Mummy

Chocolate lover,
Nasty shouter,
Chinese tiger,
Sadness scarer,
Cut healer,
Heart sharer,
Morning waker,
Council worker,
TV watcher,
Tea drinker,
Number one mother.

Robert Gordon (9)
Broughshane Primary School, Ballymena

Skipping Poem For 2010

Hydro power
Comes from the sea.
Giving me power
For my tea.

Rain, wind, sun and air
Don't cut trees, it's not fair.
Damaging the ozone you must not
Or our Earth will get hot.

Solar energy, it is good
We get energy by eating food.
No more oil, coal or gas
These fossil fuels are running out fast.

Eco-friendly, that is me
Use the sun, it is free.
We need to work as a team
To keep our Earth fresh and clean.

Emma-Lee Wray (11)
Broughshane Primary School, Ballymena

Dreams, Dreams, Dreams

Dreams, dreams, dreams
Beautiful as can be
Scream, scream, scream
Not so beautiful to me
Sweet dreams are nice
Nightmares give frights
Happy and jolly, that's a sweet dream
Scared and lonely, that's a nightmare
I would prefer sweet dreams
So cuddle your teddy tight and forget about fear
Think of nice things and sleep without tears.

Josh Houston (10)
Broughshane Primary School, Ballymena

Mrs H

Mrs H comes to school in her purple Porsche,
She is so funny,
Mrs H, you have a caring and loving heart,
I try my best to do good work for you.

Mrs H, I love the way you give us yum-yums,
She is so kind and considerate in so many ways,
I can come to you with all my problems,
Whenever I feel down.

She is eco-friendly,
In everything she does,
She loves to read
And teach poetry.

Mrs H, when I go to high school
I will miss you so much,
So I took the time to write
This poem for you!

Caitlin Lennon (11)
Broughshane Primary School, Ballymena

My Pet Dog

Fast runner
Game player
Ball burster
Loud growler
Enemy fighter
Funny footballer
Crazy footballer
Mad eater
Teddy killer
Bad swimmer
Tennis ball taker.

David Hamilton (9)
Broughshane Primary School, Ballymena

Skipping Rhyme For 2010

Keep it up
Don't fill with sorrow
Think what it'll look like
Tomorrow

Don't you care?
Can't you see?
Keep it going
Better it will be

Please don't litter
It's a waste
You won't do it
If you have taste

Bio-degradable
Energy
Stop putting waste
In the sea.

Thomas Ferguson (11)
Broughshane Primary School, Ballymena

Nice Smells

I like the smell of red roses growing in a garden,
A cooker cooking in a café baking a cake,
Perfume spraying everywhere in the room,
Honey; sweet and sugary,
Nice juicy apples from my friend's apple tree,
Fresh shampoo on my hair,
Vanilla ice cream, cold, ready to eat,
Chocolate as it melts on the stove
Ready to decorate moist cake.
I like the smell of my mum's candles
Burning on a Friday night, after a long week at school.

Jodie Hanna (8)
Broughshane Primary School, Ballymena

Skipping Game For 2010

1, 2, 3
4 and 5
Animal friendly
Stay alive

Nice clean air
Waste-free sea
Litterless grounds
Fun for me

Eco-friendly
Nice clean sea
The world's a nice
Place to be

Grow your own vegetables
Carrots for tea
Recycle paper
Save the tree!

Emma Purdy (11)
Broughshane Primary School, Ballymena

Pongs . . . Smell Bad

I hate the smell of my brother's smelly socks
Because they smell so bad, like out-of-date eggs.
I also hate the smell of my dog Arnie
After he's been rolling in mud.
And I hate the smell of an old people's home,
It smells of green vegetables and newspapers.
I also hate the smell of people smoking near me,
It stinks!
I hate the smell of old coffee,
That smell has been in the same cup for days.

Emma Catherine Speirs (9)
Broughshane Primary School, Ballymena

Smells

I love the smell of my mum's new perfume
When she sprays it on me.
I love the smell of chocolate
When I rip off the wrapper.
I love the smell of my nana's roast beef dinner
When she opens the kitchen door on a Sunday afternoon.
I love the smell of chocolate ice cream
When I walk into an ice cream shop.
I love the smell of tomato soup
When my mum puts it out on the table for my lunch on a Saturday.
I love the smell of my mum's hairspray
When she sprays it on me.
I love the smell of new books
When I walk into a library.
I love the smell of new shoes
When I walk into a shoe shop to get new shoes.

Erin Douglas (9)
Broughshane Primary School, Ballymena

Chocolate

I love to eat chocolate,
I eat it every day,
The best thing about chocolate is the taste of it.
My mum says it is bad for me
But I just walk away.
My favourite chocolate is Galaxy,
It melts on my tongue.
I love the feel of it going down my throat.
When I buy it I smell and smell it.
The chocolate I don't like I just give away.
I don't like to give chocolate away
But I just have to.

Daniel Lynn (9)
Broughshane Primary School, Ballymena

My Dog

I have a dog,
Her name is Sasha.
She's so cute and furry and is so cuddly.
She's so silly,
The way she runs around the field
And stealing other dogs bones.
She's always messing around,
A real little rascal she is.
She's funny and energetic
And always makes me laugh.
She's small in size
But has attitude.
She loves bones and treats
And is sad when she has none.
I love my dog Sasha
And she loves me!

Caitlin Caldwell (11)
Broughshane Primary School, Ballymena

Dreams

Dreams can be short
Or long
Fast or slow
Full of colours or
Black and grey
Dreams can be scary
Or funny
Happy or sad
As you wake or
In the night
Some you remember
Most you try to forget.

Rhys Frew (9)
Broughshane Primary School, Ballymena

An Autumn Breeze

The autumn breeze gushes
Through the trees
Lifting leaves on its way,
The hedgehog huddles into a clamp of leaves,
Leaving small traces behind,
The damp leaves crackling
And blowing high into the sky,
Not a sound can be heard
For all animals are asleep,
The hooting of the owls
Is carried by the wind,
The deciduous trees start swaying,
Harvest time has finally come,
The hedgehog nudges out
Once more, now winter is approaching.

Rebecca Marcus (10)
Broughshane Primary School, Ballymena

My Dog

My dog, Woody, is very cute
But sometimes he acts silly
When on his walking route.

His favourite game is throw and fetch,
He loves to run and catch the ball
Especially when it lands in the lake.

The colour of his hair is gold
But my mum says he should be sold.
He loves to fight, but doesn't bite
And at the end of the day I tell him, 'Goodnight.'

Woody is the best dog . . .
In the world.

Amy Stirling (9)
Broughshane Primary School, Ballymena

About Me

Cheryl Cole lover
Loud singer
A footballer
A midfielder
Person carer
Chelsea all over
Fast runner
An exerciser
Song writer
School hater
Good eater
Home lover
Neat writer
Science worker.

Daniel Thomas McCalmont (9)
Broughshane Primary School, Ballymena

Chocolate

I hate the smell of chocolate
Because it reminds me of my dad's brown sweaty socks,
After he has had a long day at work.

I hate the taste of chocolate
Because it tastes like a colouring pencil,
Hard and chewy.

I hate the feel of chocolate,
It's muddy when you touch it for a long time.
It melts like sticky glue in-between your fingers.

Chocolate looks like the keyboard of a computer
When I have lots of hard work to do.

I hate chocolate because it makes me feel sick.

Kirill Sakharov (8)
Broughshane Primary School, Ballymena

Imagine, Imagine

Imagine, imagine if we could live on Mars
And we all drove jet-powered cars!
Imagine, imagine if we had superpowers
And we could turn rocks into chocolate bars.
Imagine, imagine if we could fly
And no one would ever die.

Imagine, imagine if we met aliens
Who only ate geraniums!
Imagine, imagine if they spoke like cows
And never had any rows.
Imagine, imagine they told us the secret
To world peace and all our problems
Would cease!

Rachel Fleming (9)
Broughshane Primary School, Ballymena

Mmm . . . Smells Good

Mmm, I love the smell of dairy milk chocolate;
I love it melting in my mouth.
I also love the smell of freshly baked chocolate chip cookies,
As the smell drifts through the room.
The smell is great when black coffee
Dribbles out of the coffee machine.
One of my favourite smells is my mum's Sunday dinner
With some big thick carrots that slide through my teeth.
The smell is delightful when my mum
Brings a home-made pizza out of the oven.
I love the smell of huge horses
As I step out of the car into the riding stables.

Mmm . . . smells good!

Lucy McCormill (9)
Broughshane Primary School, Ballymena

Mum

Coffee drinker
Chocolate stealer
Sleepy snoozer
Flower picker
Book reader
Sparkling cleaner
Car driver
Silly mother
Messy eater
Great speller
A loud speaker
A weird swimmer
Picky eater.

Lois Smyrell (8)
Broughshane Primary School, Ballymena

A Skipping Game For 2010

Burning fossil fuels
No thank you
We'll run out
So will you.

Nuclear waste
At the bottom of the sea
Not a good idea
I think you'll agree.

Recycled paper
All the way!
It saves the trees
And it saves me!

David Stevenson (10)
Broughshane Primary School, Ballymena

There's A Monster Under My Bed!

I was in my bed
At half-past 10
I heard a thud
Under my bed

There was a monster
A very big one too
He was purple
And also very hairy

I screamed at him
He screamed at me
He said hello
I wasn't scared anymore.

Lucinda Wiley (10)
Broughshane Primary School, Ballymena

Winter

Winter's here, let's all cheer,
The holidays have begun,
We play in the snow all day long,
Ducking and dodging snowballs,
We build snowmen all day long,
But they always melt away,
People having fun going down hills in sleighs,
But no fun pulling them up,
We love to play in the snow,
Even when it's so cold.

Andrew McKee (10)
Broughshane Primary School, Ballymena

The Lonely Saddle

The saddle looked so lonely hanging there.
In a flashback I saw him once again,
Running as wild as the wind.
His inky black soft coat shining in the sun.
I could feel its silkiness underneath my fingers.
I remembered his big soft eyes
And the way they looked at me while I stroked his nose.
Now the saddle is always cold,
The leather dull and lifeless.
Maybe one day I'll have another pony.

Grace McNeill (10)
Broughshane Primary School, Ballymena

What's For Tea?

Deep in the creepy, freaky woods,
A spider is waiting, just waiting
For his prey to approach,
It's hoping for a fly or a juicy roach.
While it spins its silky golden trap,
There's no time to lose, no time to nap.
Day after day the rain pours down,
Poor little spider can't remove his frown.
There's no sign of breakfast, dinner or tea
Nothing scrummy to fill him with glee.

Shane Gibson (11)
Broughshane Primary School, Ballymena

Imagine

Imagine if it rained chocolate.
Imagine if your house was made of marshmallows.
Imagine if snow was ice cream.
Imagine if hailstones were sweets.

Imagine if water was candyfloss.
Imagine if fast food was free.
Imagine if a table was chocolate.
Imagine if vegetables tasted good.

Things are so much better in my imagination.

Jamie Wray (9)
Broughshane Primary School, Ballymena

Rocking, Popping Lemonade

Fizzy lemonade, sugary and sweet,
Tickling my taste buds as it goes past my lips.
When I open fizzy lemonade
It fizzes up and makes me jump.
Fizzy lemonade feels like bubbles exploding
Like a volcano in my mouth.
When fizzy lemonade is poured into a glass
It starts to fizz up and goes pop.
Fizzy lemonade, cool to drink in the summertime.

Jessica O'Neill (9)
Broughshane Primary School, Ballymena

Plane

Plane flying
In the sky
Gliding in the night
Huge.

Shannon Gillan (7)
Broughshane Primary School, Ballymena

My Best Friend Hannah

A caring lover
A squeezing hugger
A constant chatterer
A laughing stalker
A gift buyer
A future mother
A messy painter
A problem struggler
And I like her.

Chloé Alexandra Leitch (9)
Broughshane Primary School, Ballymena

Smells Good

I love the smell of ice-cold milk running down my throat,
It smells nice and creamy.
I like the smell of a spicy pineapple
When you cut it open.
I like the smell of brand new shoes,
I like to rip open the box and sniff them.
I love the smell of firelighters right from the packet,
Their smell reminds me of velvet curtains in my granny's house.
I like the smell of sweet perfume when my mum sprays it on me.

Naomi Lamont (9)
Broughshane Primary School, Ballymena

Football

A goal beggar
A good header
A ball banger
A football banner
A shin scriber
A goal striker
A mega midfielder
A ball stopper.

Lewis McDowell (8)
Broughshane Primary School, Ballymena

Imagine

Imagine that gravity was turned off.
People would be going up
Until they popped like a balloon.
You would go up into space and
See the moon, stars and sun.
And how would we come back down?
Maybe never!
I think I'll keep my gravity turned on.

Lauren Burrows (10)
Broughshane Primary School, Ballymena

If I Were A Teacher For The Day . . .

If I were teacher for the day . . .
I would take the class riding
Go to Belfast and have a lunch
And give no homework - yeah!
Paint instead of numeracy - great!
That would be the life!

Lucy Millar (8)
Broughshane Primary School, Ballymena

Imagine If . . .

Imagine if you could fly.
Imagine if you could touch the sky.
Imagine if you had lots of Mars bars.
Imagine if you had lots of fancy cars.
Imagine if you could meet the Queen.
Imagine if everybody was green.
Anything can happen,
Imagine, imagine, imagine.

Kirsty McKillop (10)
Broughshane Primary School, Ballymena

Outside In The Garden

There I was in the garden
The wind swirling round and round
I was so cold and shivering
As the rain was pouring down
The only one having fun
Was my pet Jess
I was so glad to hear
Mummy calling, 'It's supper time.'

Emma Hamilton (9)
Broughshane Primary School, Ballymena

If I Knew How To Fly . . .

If I knew how to fly . . .
I'd fly to space
I'd visit the people's park
I'd take my family for a ride
I'd fly home from school
I'd enjoy my newfound powers.

Faith Lamont (8)
Broughshane Primary School, Ballymena

If I Had A Million Pounds . . .

If I had a million pounds . . .
I would stay on my own grounds
I would live in my big house
With all my friends and my white mouse
Handbags, iPods, mobile phones
I could keep up with Mr Jones
Flying my helicopter up in the air
Oh what a life being a millionaire!

Adele Herron (8)
Broughshane Primary School, Ballymena

My Dog

Cold smeller
Sludgy painter
Funny swimmer
Fast runner
Loud barker
Paw printer
Friend maker
Big eater.

Nicola Kernohan (9)
Broughshane Primary School, Ballymena

If I Had A Million Pounds . . .

If I had a million pounds . . .
I'd buy an Aston Martin
I'd travel on a private jet
I'd go to every Beyoncé concert
I'd live in a mansion
I'd have a wonderful life!

Alastair McKee (8)
Broughshane Primary School, Ballymena

Golf

Hole putter
Ball hitter
Bag carrier
Golf stick swinger
Golf player
Ball finder
Tee finder
Fore shouter.

Ben Armstrong (8)
Broughshane Primary School, Ballymena

Dreams

Dreams are meant for sleeping,
Once upon a time.
Some dreams are in stories.
Some dreams can come true.
Some dreams contain fairies.
Some dreams contain death.
But most of all -
They contain *magic!*

Courtney Walsh (10)
Broughshane Primary School, Ballymena

If I Were Invisible . . .

If I were invisible . . .
I'd sneak up on someone
I'd come from school with no homework
I'd fly to Spain and back
I'd empty out the cookie jar
I'd have the time of my life!

Megan Wilmot (7)
Broughshane Primary School, Ballymena

Roxie The Coolest Doggie

Tail wagger,
Ball catcher,
High jumper,
Half springer,
Fast eater,
Toy robber,
Keen player,
Spider killer.

Sophie Dennison (9)
Broughshane Primary School, Ballymena

If I Were Invisible . . .

If I were invisible . . .
I'd scare my little sisters
I'd empty the sweetie jar
And when the teacher gives us homework
I will have the power!
I will hold my little dog
And they would never know
I would have the time of my life!

Chloe Church (8)
Broughshane Primary School, Ballymena

If I Had A Million Pounds . . .

If I had a million pounds . . .
I'd visit sunny Florida
I would go to Universal Studios
I'd buy a flashy sports car
My friends would envy *me!*
I'd have the time of my life.

Niall Douglas (7)
Broughshane Primary School, Ballymena

Football

A great kicker
A super saver
A fast runner
A football lover
A jumping keeper
A freaky manager
A fantastic defender
A classic scorer.

Scott Francey (9)
Broughshane Primary School, Ballymena

Mum

She's a . . .
Bedtime reader
Chocolate eater
Hug lover
Top stealer
Wash liker
Bed maker
Good cooker.

Ellen Moffett (8)
Broughshane Primary School, Ballymena

If I Were Invisible . . .

If I were invisible . . .
I'd visit Manchester United,
I'd get my baby sister back,
I'd go to Madagascar,
Eat ice creams and sunbathe all day,
I'd have the time of my life!

Connor McNeill (8)
Broughshane Primary School, Ballymena

Dreams

Dreams can be good.
Dreams can be bad.
Dreams can be mad and sometimes sad.

Dreams can be merry like a fairy.
Dreams can be jolly like a big lolly.
Dreams can be funny and go round in my tummy.

I love my sleep filled with all kinds of dreams.

Mark Thompson (10)
Broughshane Primary School, Ballymena

Imagine

Imagine if everything was made of chocolate!
You wouldn't have to put your hand in your pocket.
Imagine if everyone were spies
And they all ate pies!
Imagine if boys had pet dogs
And girls had frogs.
That would be such fun!

Jamie Houston (9)
Broughshane Primary School, Ballymena

Dog

Bone eater
Outside peer
Underwear stealer
Toilet drinker
Messy feeder
Loud barker
Shoe chewer.

Heather Balmer (8)
Broughshane Primary School, Ballymena

The Beast

There in the centre of a deep, dark, dreary forest,
As the wind howled through the cold restless trees,
A pair of red fiery eyes appeared in the bushes,
They were staring at me,
Like an eagle about to catch its prey,
I moved forward slightly and the eyes followed me,
And then it pounced . . .

Laura Craig (9)
Broughshane Primary School, Ballymena

Dreamland

Imagine floating slowly into the soft, fluffy clouds.
Your mind relaxes and you start to doze off.
Everything around you starts to settle down.
You dream of raining chocolate,
Pink shoes, fast cars, cute dogs, cool games.
You wake up and say . . .
'I love my very own dreamland!'

Courtney Lewis (10)
Broughshane Primary School, Ballymena

Tastes Good

I like the taste of chocolate, it runs down your throat.
I love the taste of lemonade, it pops and crackles.
I like milkshake, when it swirls around it's yummy.
I love the way lollies twirl around in your mouth.
I like it when jelly wobbles on the spoon.
I love it when ice cream just suddenly melts on my cone.
When Coke pops in your mouth it tickles, he, he, he!

Rebeka Church (8)
Broughshane Primary School, Ballymena

All Aboard the Poetry Express

If I Were Invisible . . .

If I were invisible . . .
I would raid the sweet jar
I would scare my sister
I would be a ghost
I'd visit my friend's house in secret
I'd listen to conversations
What a time I'd have!

Oscar Robinson (8)
Broughshane Primary School, Ballymena

If I Were Invisible . . .

If I were invisible . . .
I would sneak up on my cousin
I'd lock my brother up
I'd eat all the yummy sweets
I'd hide the remote from my sister
I'd play on the computer all day
Teacher would never know!

Kate Hamilton (7)
Broughshane Primary School, Ballymena

If I Were Invisible . . .

If I were invisible . . .
I'd stay at home on a school day.
I'd empty the sweet jar.
I'd scare people to bits, ha-ha.
I'd travel free on a plane to Spain.
I'd paint my brother's nose, ha-ha.
I'd have the time of my life!

Josh Balmer (8)
Broughshane Primary School, Ballymena

If I Had A Million Pounds . . .

If I had a million pounds . . .
I'd buy a DSI for *me!*
I would buy a Golf car
I would fly to Spain myself
I would buy a laptop just for *me!*
I'd have no money left!

Lydia McMullan (8)
Broughshane Primary School, Ballymena

Nightmares

Nightmares are scary,
They turn your world upside down.
I have had one about a clown.
It was scary, too scary for words.
I woke up and said to myself,
'It's OK, you're alright.'

Alyssa Alexander (9)
Broughshane Primary School, Ballymena

If I Had A Million Pounds . . .

If I had a million pounds . . .
I'd buy two puppies and two hamsters
I'd buy a big house
I'd go to LA and Asia
I'd help save people in Haiti
I would have a great life!

Lucy Gibson (7)
Broughshane Primary School, Ballymena

Robins

Robin
Red breast
Very big legs
A very sweet singer
Tall.

James Gordon (7)
Broughshane Primary School, Ballymena

Sounds Good

Gliding - the birds up above
Fluttering - the birds pass by
Roaring - the big plane passing by
Bumping - the plane landing
Cheeping - the loud noise of the birds.

Stuart McNeill (8)
Broughshane Primary School, Ballymena

Boom And Crash

Flapping - flying birds
Whistling - singing birds
Roaring - plane landing
Splashing - waves
Crunching - chocolate.

Sam Frew (8)
Broughshane Primary School, Ballymena

Birds

Fly
Eat worms
Have webbed feet
Sing in the morning
Wing.

Leah Gillan (7)
Broughshane Primary School, Ballymena

Sounds Good

Roaring - the sound of the helicopter
Bumping - the sound of the aeroplane landing
Rumbling - the sound of the rocket blasting
Twitting - of the birds singing
Buzzing - of the bees humming.

Matthew Bruce Grimsley (7)
Broughshane Primary School, Ballymena

Robin

Robin
Red breast
On the hedge
Up in the sky
Rushing.

Robert Boyd (7)
Broughshane Primary School, Ballymena

Robin

Robin
Red breast
Good at singing
Tamest of garden birds
Cute.

Jamie Alexander (8)
Broughshane Primary School, Ballymena

Robin Red Breast

Robin
Flying
In the sky
Most tamest garden bird
Graceful.

Amy Murray (8)
Broughshane Primary School, Ballymena

Robin

Robin
Red breast
Down the lane
Sits on the hedge
Lovely.

Robert O'Neill (7)
Broughshane Primary School, Ballymena

Robin

Robin
Red breast
Very long legs
Has a sweet voice
Red.

Timothy Brown (7)
Broughshane Primary School, Ballymena

Robin

Robin
Red breast
On the tree
Singing on the tree
Robin.

Jamie Knox (7)
Broughshane Primary School, Ballymena

Butterfly

Butterfly
In a cocoon
He's trapped in
He can't get out
Frightened.

Rachel Greer (8)
Broughshane Primary School, Ballymena

Planes

Planes
Are sweeping
Through the air
Hear the engine ringing
Loud.

Laura Kernohan (7)
Broughshane Primary School, Ballymena

Planes

Planes
In air
Gliding in air
And lots of birds
Flying.

Jake Nicoletti (8)
Broughshane Primary School, Ballymena

Rooks

Rooks
Flying high
Over the trees
In the playground now
Stealing.

Ben Purdy (7)
Broughshane Primary School, Ballymena

Cavan

One day I was in Cavan,
Playing my favourite sport javelin.
In my cousin's bright large house,
Where they have a big cosy couch.
They used to have two big dogs,
Beside the fire, they've a bucket of logs.
Then I'd go shopping in Cavan town,
Wondering if I'd see Mrs Brown.
Then I'd go home and have a rest,
Shopping in Cavan Town, felt the best.
Half-nine, time for bed,
Then I'd cuddly my teddy Ted.
Eight o'clock time to get up,
I'd have a mug of tea, in my favourite cup.
Now we have to go back to Derry,
But we never got to see Berry.
This new car feels a lot larger,
Mam, I accidentally forgot my mobile charger.

Jamie Cooke (11)
Culmore Primary School, Londonderry

Ten Cats

There are ten cats sitting on the roof.
There are nine that just went poof.
There are eight cats on the wall.
There are seven cats in an old house's hall.
Six cats swinging on the light.
Five of them shining bright.
Four of them are just staring into space.
Three of them are on the chase.
Two of them are just taking a nap.
And one of them just sitting on an old chap's lap.

Caitlin Greene (11)
Culmore Primary School, Londonderry

What Is Pink?
(Inspired by 'What Is Pink?' by Christina Rossetti)

What is pink? A flower is pink
In a vase in the sitting room
What is red? A car is red
Racing around a track
What is blue? The train is blue
Stopped at the station
What is white? A plane is white
Waiting on the runway to take off for Spain
What is yellow? The book is yellow
It's about trucks
What is green? A bin is green
Beside the computer in the classroom
What is violet? Wallpaper is violet
On the display board
What is orange? The paper is orange
Behind the teacher's desk.

Ronan Timlin (10)
Culmore Primary School, Londonderry

William

You are the magic in rainbows.
You are the beat in 'Beat It'.
You are the super smell of soft bacon in the pan.
You're the bubbles in Fanta, safely floating up and up.
You are like a soft fluffy bed
Keeping heat and happiness when it's dull.
You are the soft sand blowing on my feet.
You are the emotions in my heart.
You're the sun slowly drifting away.
You are the stars in the midnight sky.

Mark Bell (9)
Culmore Primary School, Londonderry

What Is Green?
(Inspired by 'What Is Pink?' by Christina Rossetti)

What is green? The grass is green
Growing around my trampoline
What is red? Roses are red
Growing in their flower bed
What is yellow? Sand is yellow
And when it blows in your eye you bellow
What is white? A page is white
And slowly turns black as you write
What is blue? The sea is blue
And it's where the fishes go through
What is orange? The sunset is orange
With a bright, bright glow that is orange
What is lemon? Why, some lemons, just some lemons.

Ava Wilson (10)
Culmore Primary School, Londonderry

A Knight's Poem
(Inspired by 'Monday's Child' poem)

Monday's knight likes a chase
Tuesday's knight will swing a mace
Wednesday's knight rescues damsels in distress
Thursday's knight will make a mess
Friday's knight likes to sing
Saturday's knight will be a king
But the knight born on the Sabbath day
Is pretty useful in every way.

Conal Gilliland (11)
Culmore Primary School, Londonderry

My Dog

You are like a blue comet travelling through the night sky.
You are like the song 'Poison'.
You're like cheesy chips and cheese pizza.
You are the best dog ever.
When you're cold you fizz like Coke.
You're like the colour of General Grevious' armour
From 'Star Wars Clone Wars'.
You are like Derry, so hard to find.
You are going to be my best friend forever.

Mathew Agavriloaie (8)
Culmore Primary School, Londonderry

What Is The Sea?

The sea is a calm blue sky.
The sea is God's happy tears.
The sea is lines of light blue paint.
The sea is a blue background to a play.
The sea is an endless adventure of water.
The sea is the raindrops that drip from Heaven.
The sea is the road for many boats.
The sea is an exciting mystery.

Emerald Jane Hockley (10)
Culmore Primary School, Londonderry

Tommy

You are like the colour blue in the sky.
You are like me listening to Green Day in my bedroom.
You are like tasting pizza on a Friday night.
You are like drinking Coca-Cola.
You are like wearing my blue and white shirt.

Eorann Ryan Griffin (8)
Culmore Primary School, Londonderry

Eila

You are like the bright blue water on a sunny day in France.
You are like listening to Abba singing on my dad's radio.
You are like eating yummy duck and pancake at the Chinese.
You are like having friends over for a sleepover.
You are like the fizzy bubbles in my delicious Sprite.
You are like the soft silk of my cosy PJs.
You are like jumping off the water trampoline in Kerry.

Cara Gilliland (8)
Culmore Primary School, Londonderry

Jack

You're like the blue and white stripe in my bedroom.
You are like pop on my CD.
You are like the chips in Fiorentini's.
You are the last sip of Coke in my glass.
You are wearing an Everton shirt.
You are in Liverpool watching Everton vs Hull City.
You are shouting when Everton score a goal.

Jack Twells (9)
Culmore Primary School, Londonderry

What Is The Moon?

The moon is a big rock floating in space.
The moon is a big yellow face looking at me.
The moon is a reflection of the sun up in the sky.
The moon is a big yellow jelly in the air.
The moon is a big piece of cheese.
The moon is a yellow dinghy sailing across the sea.

Orrian Quigley (9)
Culmore Primary School, Londonderry

Mum

You are like the colour blue.
You are like listening to 'Mamma Mia'.
You taste like chips from McDonald's.
You are like tasting juice because you are like fruit juice.
You are like wearing my secret dress
Because it feels very cosy.

Niamh Doherty (7)
Culmore Primary School, Londonderry

My Cat Seamus

You're like my purple and gold bedroom.
You are like the sunlight shining through my bedroom window.
You're like the wind and mist running past me
As I stand on the cliff in Scotland.
You are like the gold at the bottom of a rainbow.
You're like the music disco lights playing in my room.

Abbey Kinsella (9)
Culmore Primary School, Londonderry

Mum

You are like the colour green that I see in the trees.
You are like listening to JLS when I am in the bedroom.
You are the taste of a hot dog.
You are like tasting Sprite because it feels fizzy.
You are like wearing a woolly jumper because it feels soft.

Jarvis Bell (7)
Culmore Primary School, Londonderry

Eorann

You're like the first bite of corn on the cob,
With the butter running down my cheek.
You're like the greenest room in the world.
You're like the best cup in the world.
You're like the biggest birthday in the solar system.

Tommy Orr (8)
Culmore Primary School, Londonderry

My Dog Tiny

You are like the colour lilac in the sky.
You are like listening to Cheryl Cole in my bedroom.
You are the taste of pasta.
You are like tasting Coke because you bubble.
You are like wearing my spotty dress because it feels nice.

Chiara Fiorentini (8)
Culmore Primary School, Londonderry

Horses And Ponies

Cheeky Shetlands stealing scarves from their owners
Fluffy unicorns doing magic in the grassy fields
Hungry ponies munching red juicy apples
Beautiful Pegasus ponies flying high in the sky
Crafty Pegacorns galloping on white fluffy clouds
Fast Palaminos cantering to the finish line.

Courtney Annett (10)
Donegall Road Primary School, Belfast

The Love Poem

Red roses placed in their vase.
Nice perfume hugging my neck.
Loving romance whispering in my ear.
Warm kisses touching my lips.
Kind cards opened to my eyes.
Sweet chocolates melting in my mouth.

Darrel Williams (10)
Donegall Road Primary School, Belfast

Space, The Final Frontier!

Shiny rockets flying from Earth to Mars,
Tall astronauts jumping through space,
Shiny sun burning from theirs to ours,
Slimy aliens shooting, wanting to destroy the human race,
Shiny stars shooting through time and space.

Carl McGrath (10)
Donegall Road Primary School, Belfast

Football

Dirty keepers diving trying to save the player's shots.
Rough players kicking and sliding on the ground.
Skillful Rooney skills around Torres.
Sweaty striker scoring goals.
Loud crowds singing, 'Come on you Reds!'

Corin Henry (10)
Donegall Road Primary School, Belfast

Liverpool Mad

Fast Gerrard kicking the ball into the net.
Angry Benitez walking away on the players.
Angry Ngog hit Kuyt because he was annoyed.
Hairy players pass the ball so they can strike.
Sweaty players stink out the dressing room.

Rebecca Harrison (10)
Donegall Road Primary School, Belfast

The Football Match

Sweaty football players stink out the changing room.
Wet crowd cheers for the goalkeeper.
Loud Fernando Torres falls to the ground.
Tall goalkeeper saves the goals.
Dirty kits jumping off people.

Alannah Gilliland (9)
Donegall Road Primary School, Belfast

Poetry Express

I
Am going
On a trip
A very, very long
Trip, off to the North
Pole, I go with my snow
Dogs, it is very cold
I meet Santa and
Stay for a
Nice little
Chat.

Leah Barrons (10)
Eden Primary School, Carrickfergus

My Journey

I
am going
to Peru today.
I will meet Paddington
Bear and his aunt Lucy.
I am getting on the plane.
Boom, boom, crash, I have arrived. Wow!
I go to the Brown's house
in London. There is Paddington
in the middle of
the room, I
am in
now.

Rachel Moore (10)
Eden Primary School, Carrickfergus

Back In Time

Back in time I want to go,
And now I want to know,
'Cause I forgot what life's like without a sister,
Keke, the giraffe, took my mind off a blister.

Into my granny and granda's house for hours,
Now I go home in Granda's car.

Time in the war my granda said was scary,
It was lovely, my granny's nickname was Mary,
My mummy and me bake a cake,
Every time it is hard to make.

Louise Shields (10)
Eden Primary School, Carrickfergus

School Tour

S weets we have to pack
C hoose the right ones
H op in the car
O ff to school we go
O n the bus to take us to the boat
L et's get on the boat and sail

T o Scotland, let's have lots of fun
O ur heads are spinning on the roller coaster
U mbrellas up, it's starting to rain
R ain, who cares? Let's have fun.

Heather Briers (10)
Eden Primary School, Carrickfergus

Madagascar

M agic and joy with laughter and friends are better
A nd if you go there you will have lots of fun
D ance with friends
A nd have fun
G ames and toys for us
A nd have a good day
S ave your money
C ar to get there
A nimals live there
R ide on a lion and it is like a zoo.

Demi-Louise Harper (9)
Eden Primary School, Carrickfergus

My Journey To Paris

D isneyland Paris
I ce lollies to eat
S unny days in Paris
N ice people to talk to
E ndless amount of rides to go on
Y ou go with friends, it's better
L aughing at funny jokes
A nimals so cool
N ever to go home
D isneyland is so much fun.

Anna Coulter (9)
Eden Primary School, Carrickfergus

My Trip To Tesco

I am going to Tesco,
I am going in my own car,
It is very, very hot.

There are a lot of people,
I first need to go to the toy aisle,
It's a nightmare in here.

I need some Coco Pops,
They are now on sale,
Hooray!

Victoria Phillips (10)
Eden Primary School, Carrickfergus

The Future

T o the future I go,
H earing new things,
E ating new things.

F ood is terrible,
U mbrellas are gone,
T eachers are evil,
U p the years I go,
R eally it is nothing like what I imagined,
E ducation is bad, that's not good for us.

Joel Colligan (10)
Eden Primary School, Carrickfergus

ASDA

Let's
All go
To ASDA to
Get some healthy pasta
I hear it's very hippy
It was just one
Pound sixty, now
It's one
Fifty.

Sam Lilburn (10)
Eden Primary School, Carrickfergus

Mars

M ars is amazing, I'm glad I'm here,
A stronauts are jealous because they're not me,
R eal Martians live on Mars,
S o I'm the first person on Mars.

Scott Nichol (10)
Eden Primary School, Carrickfergus

Amazing Australia

A nice sunny day
U nable to stop wandering
S un shining all day
T iring but fun
R unning in the sun
A lways in the desert
L icking ice cream
I always have fun
A long tiring day.

Emily Jane Iles (10)
Eden Primary School, Carrickfergus

Cool Caribbean

C ycling around you can see:
A ll the food is lovely.
R eally exciting.
I t's in the sea.
B rilliant beaches.
B irds look pretty.
E xotic wildlife.
A really good place.
N owhere is boring.

Rebecca Reid (10)
Eden Primary School, Carrickfergus

Orlando

O ur family are going to Orlando.
R an to the car in Orlando.
L eft house to go to Disney World.
A t 12.45pm we got home.
N ow we are going home.
D own the plane went, we were in Northern Ireland.
O ur house was spotless.

Nathan Christopher Adams (10)
Eden Primary School, Carrickfergus

Viking

V ikings had armour like Romans did but were more vicious
I think that the longship idea was great
K ings were not liked then because they always did the wrong things
I think the ice skates were cool
N ow we love them but they used to be feared
G ood people like monks fought back but weren't successful.

Corey Steele (9)
Eden Primary School, Carrickfergus

Ireland!

I rish dancing!
R iver dance!
E ntertainment!
L ovely music!
A mazing!
N ice footwear!
D resses!

Kristen Kavanagh (10)
Eden Primary School, Carrickfergus

Future

F lying cars are floating around me.
U nderground there is a home for robots.
T ests are run on your brain.
U nderground there also is a hotel for robots.
R obot people are walking around.
E lephants have rocket feet to fly with.

Joshua Lee Johnston (9)
Eden Primary School, Carrickfergus

Space

S pectacular sights of Earth and Mars
P robes of space look like space cars
A liens surely don't exist, do they?
C rumbling space junk clutters the sky
E xciting events lie nearby.

David Seaman (10)
Eden Primary School, Carrickfergus

Disneyland Paris

P laying out in the sun and in the swimming pool
A t Disneyland Paris I will buy things
R unning and getting exercise in the sun
I will play with my friends if I get any
S tay in Disneyland Paris for two weeks.

Katie Louise Patterson (9)
Eden Primary School, Carrickfergus

What Will Happen In The Future?

Flying cars?
Superpowers?
Massive flowers?
Musical towers?
Visiting Mars?

Who knows?

Purple trees?
Chocolate cheese?
Fishy fees?
Scarlet peas?
Spotty bees?

Who knows?

Movable houses?
Talking trousers?
Walking blouses?
Dancing mouses?
Funky grouses?

Who knows?

Lime-green skies?
Electric pies?
Moaning flies?
Stripy guys?
Strawberry fries?

Who knows?

Life in the future,
The truth really is,
No one knows,
We can only guess!

Who knows?

Peter Forde (11)
Irish Society's Primary School, Coleraine

My Adventure Holiday!

On my adventure holiday
I ate my breakfast on a silver tray
Because I was acting as the Queen
I saw politicians looking mean
I was a famous explorer, exploring far and wide
My name was Barteny Hardly Tride
I went to the Sahara desert and
Explored among the sand
    I went to explore the Amazon
    This time I was Carteny Flynn
    I escaped the deadly crocodiles
    That were the vilest of the vile
On my adventure holiday
I met a super detective called Cray
He had a mask over his face
And was on an undercover case
    I followed him into the dark, dark night
    And watched him have a gruesome fight
    With a villain called Slythery Slack
    He gave up - hid behind a rubbish stack
On my adventure holiday
I met a detective who was called Cray
I went to explore the Amazon
And my name was Carteny Flynn
    I went exploring far and wide
    My name was Barteny Hardly Tride
    I saw politicians looking mean
    When I was acting as the Queen
I did a lot today
On my adventure holiday.

Natasha Brownlee (11)
Irish Society's Primary School, Coleraine

Under The Deep Blue Sea

There are things to do and things to see
There are places to go and places to see
But the place I must see
Is the deep blue sea
The fish that swim in a shoal
They are better to watch than burning coal
The crabs that walk from side to side
While other fish are trying to hide
The whales that swim so slow
While other fish start to show
Some fish can be big and tall
But others can be thin and small
The different sorts of fish
Have all become a popular dish
But what people don't know
Is where they all go
Do they swim for fun
Or do they like the sparkle of the sun?
When a shark attacks do some survive?
That's what I want to know when I go to dive
Where do they go on cold days?
Do they all go different ways?
There are things to do and things to see
There are places to go and places to see
But the place I must see
Is under the deep blue sea.

Grace Rosborough (11)
Irish Society's Primary School, Coleraine

Shark Attack

Teeth gnasher
Bone smasher
Distinctive sniffer
Blood whiffer
Fish pursuer
Chaos brewer
Real killer
Not a thriller
Deadly biter
Strong fighter
Teeth gripper
Sharp nipper
Meat eater
Death cheater
Skeleton cruncher
Plankton muncher
Ocean ruler
Blood drooler
Saltwater lover
Hunts undercover
Sea quaker
Tail shaker
Captor eluder
Unwelcome intruder.

Rosanna Aimee Johnston (10)
Irish Society's Primary School, Coleraine

Home

H ome is very nice,
O ld but awesome,
M y body can relax,
E verywhere at home!

Kent Morton (10)
Irish Society's Primary School, Coleraine

Under The Sea

When I look out to sea
I often wonder what would I see
If I could go under the sea
I wonder what there could be
I'm sure there are many creatures under the sea
Big, small, oh what are we
Compared to those creatures under the sea?
I often wonder what they eat
One sure thing is they like their meat
From a very large shark, to a small sea horse
They get all they need under the sea
Monday, Tuesday, Wednesday, Thursday, Friday,
Saturday, Sunday
Seven days in a week
I'm sure when they see each other
They think there is no other, as they think
They look like a freak to each other
I'm sure it's dark under the sea
Not a place for you or me
Believe me I wouldn't like to be under the sea.

Brett Wade (11)
Irish Society's Primary School, Coleraine

Back In Time

If I went back in time
I wouldn't start to rhyme,
But go and see the dinosaurs
And see if they were so bad.
It would probably be the best time I ever had.
I'd go and see the cavemen,
They're meant to be barking mad,
Probably just like us!

Aaron Millar (10)
Irish Society's Primary School, Coleraine

Under The Sea

What could there be?
Big fish and little fish
And tails that go swish
But there's only the one
That's lovely and fun.
It's the smartest mammal you can get
Have you guessed who he is yet?
Yes, a dolphin it is
He is certainly a quick whizz
But when you get past
The spiky pufferfish
And the deadly cuttlefish
There is one that is last
And very, very fast,
It is the great white shark
That's gonna leave a mark!
Now I've told you about the fish
Now my wish
Has come true
To write a poem just for you.

Amy Allen (10)
Irish Society's Primary School, Coleraine

Dinosaurs!

Dinosaurs! Dinosaurs!
Oh! I love it when you munch on liver
And slither!
You crawl and fall
All because you're a bone cruncher
And a homework muncher.
That's why I love you
Dinosaur! *Roar!*

Ethan Kelly (10)
Irish Society's Primary School, Coleraine

My View On The World

Up, up and away I go
Floating away so slowly
The birds are singing in my ears
And I am laughing contentedly

Everywhere I look there's
Something interesting to see
The hills, the beaches, the sky
Are filled with such wonderful things

I'm on my way down now
Everything is becoming clearer
I've nearly landed
Oh I'm so near

The grass is becoming greener
And I can see my mum waiting
For me in the crowd that's getting
Nearer and nearer and nearer

Oh the world is such an exciting place.

Victoria Lynch (11)
Irish Society's Primary School, Coleraine

Scaly Fish

S lippery fish are
C old even on the hottest places on Earth like
A frica, it looks
L ike they talk about my favourite colour
Y ellow but I don't think you get yellow.

F ish, I had a fish called
I saac but he was
S ilvery grey but
H e is a famous fish now because he turned yellow!

Saima Asghar (10)
Irish Society's Primary School, Coleraine

An Adventure Above!

I would love to ride up to the sky!
Fly away with my magic unicorn,
Jump on the cotton candy and eat it while I go,
See the universe so big, filled with many delights,
Asking my unicorn if something can be so
And that is to turn something good into pure winter snow!
I say marshmallows, I say clear crystals,
This is a secret I will never reveal.

I'll go even higher, higher, and higher!
Until I reach a magical waterfall,
It quenches your thirst and runs down the streaming trees,
Though now it turns violet and that means evil approaches, so I'll retreat,
Then I'll go even higher, really high!
To a galaxy of stars, where the sun beams out to the Earth
And shines like a golden orb, and the planets represent it and treat it like royalty,
Where the moon is full and wonderful and it's where I long to be.

Anna McKeown (10)
Irish Society's Primary School, Coleraine

Killer Whale

I'm a killer whale
I live in the sea
I have a hole on top of me.

I am a mammal
And I like to swim deep
But I come up to the surface to sleep.

I have no arms or legs, not even feet
But I have a big tail
Which follows behind me on a trail.

Olivia Marshall (10)
Irish Society's Primary School, Coleraine

Under The Sea!

The sea is blue
The baby dolphins are new.
They jump out of the sea so high
As if they can fly!

The scuba divers
Are great survivors.
They search for sea creatures
And oh boy do they have some features!
They see plants and flowers
Almost the height of towers!

Rocks and stones
Are tiny fishes' homes.
They search for food
Even other fish include!

If you ever go in the sea
You'll never be alone
Because there's the perfect friend in there with me!

Amy Claire Cutler (11)
Irish Society's Primary School, Coleraine

London Eye

L ovely ride that looks
O ver all of London.
N ever before in my life had I
D one something that is so much fun
O n the right time . . .
N ight!

E veryone enjoys a
Y o-yo!
E rr . . . what does a yo-yo have to do with the London Eye?

Ben Clarke (10)
Irish Society's Primary School, Coleraine

Under The Sea

Under the sea, oh what fun
A little secret, don't tell anyone
Once I'm deep, deep down below
All the secrets begin to show

It starts with a tingle in my toes
Then with a flash to the waist it goes
My sea horse laughs, I give a twirl
I'm no longer an ordinary girl

I swim to my throne and up I get
I'm now a mermaid so don't forget
I take my crown, place it on my head
Clustered with rubies; a beautiful red

I am now the queen of the sea
So everyone rejoices with me
I've had a brilliant day so far
With my magical mermaid power.

Olivia Walker (11)
Irish Society's Primary School, Coleraine

In A Playroom

Used to be an attic
But now it is a playroom.
A quarter of it is mine
And three quarters of it is my brother's.
In a room I have a corner
And my brother has it all.
It's a cheerful place like me.
I love it a lot and always will.
The reason why I like it
Is because it's fun and airy
And it is so fun to play in.

Sarah Harte (10)
Irish Society's Primary School, Coleraine

The Dig

I found a coin which gave a glint,
It was deep down in the soil
And at history it did hint,
Scraped away with hours of toil.

It had a picture of Julius Caesar
And if you look in the books,
You will find he was a Roman Emperor,
It was worth the hours it took.

Digging at a steady pace,
Right now I'm very mucky
And in this case,
I got very lucky.

I've had a good time,
I'm happy with what I have got,
Now I've got a treasure that will always be mine
And it wasn't as easy as I thought.

Oliver Warke (11)
Irish Society's Primary School, Coleraine

My Favourite Place

I am an English seaside town
Thousands of people visit me every year
I have the tallest roller coaster in Europe
I have three Victorian piers
Miles of golden sand, tall steel tower
Dancing around on summer nights
Football ground, Bloomfield Road, different flavours of rock
I am world famous for my lights
Where am I?

A: Blackpool.

Chelsea Irwin (11)
Irish Society's Primary School, Coleraine

Fish

Fish have sparkly scales
Orange wavy tails
Fish are jelly
Not nice in your belly
Fish can fly
Fish are shy
Fish are flat
Fish can even be a cat
Fish are clowns
Fish are round
Fish are spotty
Fish are naughty
Fish are old
Fish are gold
That's the fish under the sea
Some fish are for you and me!

Emma Louise Bell (10)
Irish Society's Primary School, Coleraine

Under The Sea

Under the sea there are lots of creatures.
There is a huge shark
And a jumpy sea horse as well.
All with great features.
Oh and there is a catfish too,
I wonder if it miaows or not.
There's a stripy clownfish
And a spotty octopus too.
There is also a pufferfish.
There are quite a lot,
But my favourite sea creature is the
Very intelligent dolphin.

Chloe Rae (11)
Irish Society's Primary School, Coleraine

The Hidden Brooch

Open up my magic box
And take a peep inside
Open up my magic box
And show my story far and wide
Look I glisten!

Open up my magic box
I'm shiny, hard and cold
Open up my magic box
I must be made of gold
Look I shine!

Open up my magic box
And brush the dust aside
Open up my magic box
'It's a medieval brooch!' the archaeologist cried
Look I sparkle!

Niamh McMullan (10)
Irish Society's Primary School, Coleraine

Dinosaurs, Dinosaurs

I went back to the age of the dinosaurs,
I felt so weird.
There are many different types of the magnificent creatures,
Some are big, some are small, some are vicious, some are gentle,
But I wouldn't mess with any of them.
My favourite would have to be the Tyrannosaurus Rex
With its enormous jaws and flesh-ripping teeth,
He is the dinosaur king.
Some are herbivores, some are omnivores but Rex is a carnivore!
When I came back I was in my room
And I told my mum straight away
But of course she didn't believe me!

Michael Diamond (11)
Irish Society's Primary School, Coleraine

Sir Alex Ferguson

S tunning team
I ce baths his players love
R eady to win!

A mazing manager
L oveable legend
E very supporter worships him
eX pert he is!

F ighting for the League
E xercise he needs
R ooney's the best
G rumpy sometimes
U nique things he has done
S uch great players
O ptions on the bench
N oisy stadium!

Lewis Mitchell (11)
Irish Society's Primary School, Coleraine

My Favourite Place

My favourite place is Spain,
I fly there in a plane.
Out there I have a holiday home
And a stringy float made out of foam.
There is lots of fun stuff to do,
Like going to the water park or riding a canoe.
You can hire out a banana boat
Or even buy a blow-up float.
There are lots of shops to see
And that's where I'll have a shopping spree!
My favourite place is Spain,
I'll have to go there again!

Demi-Lee Friel (11)
Irish Society's Primary School, Coleraine

City Vs Country

City
Noisy, busy
Buzzing, wailing, collapsing
Skyscrapers, smoke, houses, cottages
Sleeping, whispering, breathing
Quiet, empty
Country.

City
Prominent, peculiar
Slipping, sliding, snatching
Competition, cars, cottages, carts
Snoozing, sleeping, snoring
Playful, peaceful
Country.

Emma Tran (11)
Irish Society's Primary School, Coleraine

Under The Sea

There are so many magical things under the sea,
Where, I wonder, could a treasure chest be?

There are some wonderful fish,
Oh, I wish I could live under the sea, oh, how I wish!

I wonder what it's like under the water,
Maybe if there was a mermaid, I could be friends with her.
Swimming around the coral reef, enjoying myself a lot!
I wish I could take some home and plant it in a pot!

I would meet so many friends down there
And also a sea creature with seaweed for hair!
I would have a home under the sea,
Oh, how wonderful it would be for me!

Danielle Mullan (10)
Irish Society's Primary School, Coleraine

The Monster In My Dreams

My favourite place is in the woods
Where would I rather be?
There are so many plants to discover and animals to see
The leaves crack and make a noise below my shaking feet
Yet they do it in such an even lovely cunning beat
With monstrous head and sickening cry
And ears like errant wings
It moves under the bushes fast
And on the trees it swings
I try to move but I cannot for I'm paralysed with fear
As the hideous creature lurks very near
Suddenly it jumps out at me with one ginormous leap
Then I find out it's all a dream and I go back to sleep.

Paulina Marszalek (10)
Irish Society's Primary School, Coleraine

The Scottish Highlands

Noisy clatter
Bird chatter
Big clatter
Streams flowing
Rivers rushing
Blowy trees
Windy whistles
Stormy clouds
Lashing rain
Thunder roarer
Lashing hailstones
Crackling mountains
Where has all the peace gone?

Macauley Whitehead (11)
Irish Society's Primary School, Coleraine

I Am Not Under The Sea

I am not under the sea
Or in the forest.

I am on an archaeologist's dig,
Looking for a headless chicken
Or maybe even a bone.

I'd rather have an ice cream cone
Than digging in the mud while hesitating.

I thought I'd go with my first idea,
Under the sea,
Let's, and see what I can see.

Sara Carr (10)
Irish Society's Primary School, Coleraine

Books

P aths leading
O ver dry deserts
E nding at lush rainforests
M ade for people
S itting in comfy chairs

P eace in my house
O verhead the clock chimes
E ntering a new world
M y wonderful world
S itting in a book.

James Hancock (10)
Irish Society's Primary School, Coleraine

Sea Creatures

S harp teeth
H eavy as a boat
A t the bottom of the sea
R uthless as a lion
K illing for some meat

F unny-looking
I ndigo sea they live in
S hark prey
H uman food.

Ryan Jamison (11)
Irish Society's Primary School, Coleraine

Tiny Fish

T eeny weeny fish
I mperceptible fish
N ot in my dish
Y ay! Go fish!

F ish are wonderful
I ncredibly colourful
S wimming from a shark
H iding in the dark.

Alexandra O'Neill (11)
Irish Society's Primary School, Coleraine

Spain

S un, sun, sun, that's all you ever see.
P laying all day long.
A place where I like to go.
I t's very, very hot.
N ext time I'll remember to bring suncream!

Alyx Campbell (10)
Irish Society's Primary School, Coleraine

My Favourite Place - Fuerteventura

Fuerteventura is a place to have fun
Out in the sun, I can scream and run.
Looking around I see happy faces
When I'm in my room unpacking my cases.

Splashing about in the pool
Trying to keep lovely and cool.
In the plane I give a big sigh
I never noticed the time fly by!

Sydney Rosier (10)
Irish Society's Primary School, Coleraine

Opposites

City
Loud, busy
Crowding, hustling, bustling
Fog, smoke, field, fences
Free, silencing, ambling
Empty, peaceful
Country.

Cavan Tayler (11)
Irish Society's Primary School, Coleraine

Dolphin

D ancing in the air
O blivious to people watching them
L ove the attention
P rofessionals at swimming
H igh as the sky
I 'll hope to see you soon
N oble, smart animals.

Robyn McCracken (11)
Irish Society's Primary School, Coleraine

My Snow Day

Across the fields it's quiet and still,
As the snow lies on the top of every hill.
When all of a sudden a great noise arises,
Much to the huge snowmen's surprises.

Snowballs are thrown out of mid-air,
Soft and round like the tail of a hare.
Screams come from left and right,
I think they're having a snowball fight.

Now on goes the light of the stars,
But still the noise can be heard from afar.
Wait, I can hear a car go *beep*,
Finally it's time for me to get some sleep.

I wake up early to see the rising of the sun,
So I decide to go outside and have some fun.
I walk out on this snowy day,
It is still very cold, I have to say.

I pick up some snow for my snowman and squish it,
And find a Canadian hat that did fit.
Then I spot my best friend Heather,
So after all we have a snowball fight together!

Hannah McCurdy (11)
Kilmoyle Primary School, Ballymoney

Snow, Oh No!

I hate it, I hate it, I hate it so,
I think it's time for the snow to go.
I trip over a big slippy mound
And then I fall to the ground.

Though it's extremely cold,
I have to go outside so I'm told
To build snowmen and play.
I can stay inside another day.

A snowball hits me, it is sore,
I wish I could run in that door.
I want there to be some sun,
How do the other children find snow fun?

My toes are freezing
And I cannot stop sneezing.
When I go into the town,
It is so icy I fall down.

The snow is turning into slush,
I hope it goes in a rush.
We'll soon forget the cold and ice,
Let's hope the summer will be nice!

Tori Ann Hartin (10)
Kilmoyle Primary School, Ballymoney

Redshank

On the mud flats
I saw you, redshank
Collecting your food for winter.

Your short fine beak
As thin as a needle.

On the mud flats
I saw you, redshank
Collecting your food for winter.

Your thin little legs
Just like a pin.

On the mud flats
I saw you, redshank
Collecting your food for winter.

Your short small wings
As short as a pencil.

On the mud flats
I saw you, redshank
Collecting your food for winter.

Ashley McBride (9)
Kilmoyle Primary School, Ballymoney

Lapwing

In the shallow water
lapwing
I saw you hopping.

Your small legs move fast
if you hear a noise.

In the shallow water
lapwing
I saw you hopping.

Your sharp beak as skinny as can be
while you look for food.

In the shallow water
lapwing
I saw you hopping.

Your silky wings
are soft and bony.

In the shallow water
lapwing
I saw you hopping.

Verity Alicia Wilson (8)
Kilmoyle Primary School, Ballymoney

Building A Snowman

As I look outside and see the snow,
To build a snowman off we go.
First of all we need a coat and hat,
On the sofa there it sat.

We went outside and made a ball,
We must be careful we do not fall.
Bigger and bigger and bigger it grows,
How big it will be no one knows.

We now shall start the snowman's head,
Beside my daddy's garden shed.
We'll put it on the other ball,
And really hope it does not fall.

We found some coal for his mouth and his eyes,
A carrot for his nose, oh what a surprise!
My dad found a scarf and hat to match,
Put them on the snowman and then it collapsed!

Tom Hayes (10)
Kilmoyle Primary School, Ballymoney

My Niece Farràh

My niece Farràh is a princess-pink,
She is summer,
In a garden of happiness,
She is a clear blue sky with a ray of sunshine,
She is a bright rainbow-coloured dress,
She is a diamond-covered throne,
She is a little Peppa Pig
And a lovely angel cake.

Chloé Gardiner (11)
Kilmoyle Primary School, Ballymoney

My Dog Oscar

I love my dog Oscar
He's always filed with glee.
But he never gets tired
As far as I can see!

If you're silly enough
He'll let you throw his ball all day
And when you finally get tired
He'll still want to play.

If he ever gets a dog bed
He'll always rip it up
But he is so cute
You can't tell him he's a naughty pup!

Oh my dog Oscar
How can you be so cute?
With ears as soft as velvet
And fur as black as soot.

Annie McIlhatton (10)
Kilmoyle Primary School, Ballymoney

I Love The Snow

I go outside to the snow,
Let's see how far these snowballs will go.
Lots of car tracks I have seen,
But outside Mum and Dad haven't been.

Lots of warm clothes I have on,
But my hat falls off and now it's gone.
Outside I bring my sliding sledge,
I slide all around pretending it is the Ice Age.

Maybe later on I can build a snowman,
As the judge I can choose my old gran.
To go skiing I would love,
But somehow I've lost my skiing glove.

But I'm glad to be at home,
The snow is soft like crafty foam.
The snow is just so good to admire,
But now it's time to go inside to the fire.

Sarah Bleakly (9)
Kilmoyle Primary School, Ballymoney

The Flow Of Snow

As I look outside and see the snow,
To build a snowman off we go.
Mum says, 'Keep warm,' I know,
She always says that when it snows.

As we go out all wrapped up,
My dog follows, we call him Pup.
I find a snowball, throw it at my brother,
Then get shouted at by my mother.

I go outside and have a run,
Watch other children having fun.
I make a ball and roll it round,
Somehow I made a giant mound.

Hot chocolate is waiting with some treats,
I really do have cold feet.
Slipping and sliding my father comes over,
Telling us the sun is down and the day is over.

Emma Creelman (10)
Kilmoyle Primary School, Ballymoney

Fun In The Snow

As I look outside and see the snow,
To build a snowman off we go.
As I go outside I blow my nose,
I hope I don't get very cold toes.

Snow is falling all around,
You can't hear it when it hits the ground.
As I run around with my friend,
I see boys skidding at every bend.

We challenge the boys to a snowball fight,
But now us girls are trembling with fright.
Now we're brave and ready to fight,
We see the boys run out of sight.

We make snow angels on the ground,
When it snows again they won't be found.
As I go inside for some hot cocoa,
I really hope the snow doesn't go, go.

Abby-Jo Johnston (10)
Kilmoyle Primary School, Ballymoney

Five Fat Gorillas!

Five fat gorillas danced on the floor
One bashed his head
And then there were four.

Four fat gorillas had a burger and tea
One went to the toilet
And then there were three.

Three fat gorillas all said, 'Moo'
One did not say it
And then there were two.

Two fat gorillas had a bun
One said, 'Yuck'
And then there was one.

One fat gorilla went crying to his mum
He went to bed
And then there were none.

Bailey Dobbin (9)
Kilmoyle Primary School, Ballymoney

Lapwing

Lapwing oh lapwing
a little picker

Lapwing oh lapwing
soaring across the sky

Eating shellfish and crabs
like we eat a fry

Lapwing oh lapwing
with eye-stabbing beak

Lapwing oh lapwing
a little picker.

Sam Dowey (9)
Kilmoyle Primary School, Ballymoney

Five Hungry Dogs

Five hungry dogs went to the shore
One got drowned
And then there were four.

Four hungry dogs went to find a key
One got locked in
And then there were three.

Three hungry dogs walked into glue
One got stuck
And then there were two.

Two hungry dogs went to have some fun
One got lost
And then there was one.

One hungry dog went to its mum
Felt sad and lonely
Then there were none.

Matthew Irons (10)
Kilmoyle Primary School, Ballymoney

Five Mad Men

Five mad men sat on the floor
One went to the shop
And then there were four

Four mad men went into the sea
One fell in
And then there were three

Three mad men all turned blue
One flew away
And then there were two

Two mad men each got a gun
One shot the other
And then there was one

One mad man was all alone
He went back home
And then there were none.

Jacob Creelman (8)
Kilmoyle Primary School, Ballymoney

Five Naughty Boys

Five naughty boys went to the shore
one ate a crab
and then there were four.

Four naughty boys ate a bee
one took a stroke
and then there were three.

Three naughty boys went to the zoo
one got scared
and then there were two.

Two naughty boys ate a bun
one got poisoned
and then there was one.

One naughty boy got badly stung
he went to hospital
and then there were none.

Sophie Howard (9)
Kilmoyle Primary School, Ballymoney

Five Silly Elephants

Five silly elephants sitting by the door
one fell over
and then there were four.

Four silly elephants climbing a tree
one branch broke
and then there were three.

Three silly elephants trying to moo
one did it wrong
and then there were two.

Two silly elephants weighing a ton
one was too fat
and then there was one.

One silly elephant went to have fun
he got lonely
and then there were none.

Joanna Christie (9)
Kilmoyle Primary School, Ballymoney

Five Fat Men

Five fat men slipped on the floor
One broke his leg
And then there were four.

Four fat men climbed up a tree
One licked a leaf
And then there were three.

Three fat men all said, *'Moo'*
One got hit
And then there were two.

Two fat men weighed a ton
One ate too much
And then there was one.

One fat man got a gun
He shot it into his lung
And then there were none.

Craig Freeman (8)
Kilmoyle Primary School, Ballymoney

Five Skinny Monkeys

Five skinny monkeys feeling very bored
One fell asleep
And then there were four.

Four skinny monkeys swinging in a tree
One fell off
And then there were three.

Three skinny monkeys went to the loo
One sat too long
And then there were two.

Two skinny monkeys with a gun
One shot the other
And then there was one.

One skinny monkey went home to his mum
Told her he was bored
And then there were none.

Matthew McClean (8)
Kilmoyle Primary School, Ballymoney

Five Silly Men

Five silly men leapt at a door
One tripped over
And then there were four.

Four silly men ate a pea
One got swine flu
And then there were three.

Three silly men went to the loo
One got stuck
And then there were two.

Two silly men ate a bun
One got too fat
And then there was one.

One silly man saw some dung
One got stunk out
Then there were none.

Johnathan Smith (9)
Kilmoyle Primary School, Ballymoney

Five Old Grannies

Five old grannies went to the shore
One got lost
And then there were four

Four old grannies paid a fee
One went mad
And then there were three

Three old grannies went to the zoo
One got a monkey
And then there were two

Two old grannies walked for fun
One fell over
And then there was one

One old granny had no lung
Then she died
And then there were none.

Lynzi Stirling (9)
Kilmoyle Primary School, Ballymoney

Five Silly Clowns

Five silly clowns getting a mower
One was knocked down
And then there were four.

Four silly clowns climbing a tree
One fell down
And then there were three.

Three silly clowns shouting *moo*
One lost his voice
And then there were two.

Two silly clowns playing with a gun
One shot himself
And then there was one.

One silly clown having a bit of fun
He tripped over me
And then there were none.

Coran Martin McCook (9)
Kilmoyle Primary School, Ballymoney

Five Silly Dogs

Five silly dogs spat on the floor
One slipped and fell
And then there were four.

Four silly dogs ate a flea
One choked himself
And then there were three.

Three silly dogs got stuck in glue
One had fun
And then there were two.

Two silly dogs ate a cream bun
One got too fat
And then there was one.

One silly dog had no fun
He was cross
And then there were none.

Victoria McKeeman (8)
Kilmoyle Primary School, Ballymoney

Five Tough Soldiers

Five tough soldiers on the floor
One went away
And then there were four.

Four tough soldiers decided to flee
One got shot
And then there were three.

Three tough soldiers got stuck in glue
One set a landmine
And then there were two.

Two tough soldiers got a gun
One killed the other
And then there was one.

One tough soldier said his job was done
He went away
And then there were none.

Lyle Kennedy (9)
Kilmoyle Primary School, Ballymoney

Curlew

In the wet sand
curlew
I saw you with your chickens
looking for food

In the wet sand
curlew
I saw you drying
your wings

In the wet sand
curlew
I saw your long legs

In the wet sand
curlew
I saw your beak so long
you don't have to bend down.

Travis Kane (10)
Kilmoyle Primary School, Ballymoney

Super Cars

The Lamborghini Murcielago,
With its brilliant orange paint
And the Porsche 911 turbo,
It's so awesome you could nearly faint.

The fastest car in the world was the speedy McLaren F1
Until one miraculous day,
The Bugatti Veyron was born!

Flying down the road in my Audi R8,
When you're reaching its speed limit it feels just great.
The Ferrari Enzo, what a car,
Good job it has a roll bar.

Jack Dowey (11)
Kilmoyle Primary School, Ballymoney

Me Moving At School

I sing and smile,
I type and tie,
I dart, draw and dance.
I read and rub,
I whisper and write
And frequently I prance.

I jig and jog,
I talk and think,
I work, walk and write.
I clink and clap,
I leap and learn
And now and then -
I fight.

Lois Carson (9)
Kilmoyle Primary School, Ballymoney

Four Little Monkeys

Four little monkeys in a tree
One fell and broke his leg
Then there were three

Three little monkeys went to the zoo
One fed the lion
And then there were two

Two little monkeys ate a bun
One found a flea
And then there was one

One little monkey shot himself with a gun
Then he was dead
And then there were none.

Ellie McAlister (8)
Kilmoyle Primary School, Ballymoney

Building A Snowman

As I look outside and see the snow,
To build a snowman off we go.
For today is the best day,
So let's have some fun whilst we play.

Let's wrap up warm, remember it's cold,
Yes Mum, I know, I've already been told.
Start with the head, roll it into a ball,
But we have to be careful, it might just fall.

The smiles on our faces say we're having fun,
But just look at our snowman, he's very nearly done.
We shout, 'He's finished!' with a smile,
Let's go inside to rest a while.

Molly Elder (10)
Kilmoyle Primary School, Ballymoney

Snow

As we look and see the snow,
To build a snowman off we go.
It looks very cold,
'Wrap up warm,' we are told.

We start having a snowball fight,
It gives an old lady a *big* fright.
A little boy falls and hurts his bum,
Now he's crying for his mum!

We all start building a snow pile,
One of the boys thought we could build it for a mile!
Mum's shouting, 'Time to go,
Before you freeze up like the snow!'

Timothy Keys (10)
Kilmoyle Primary School, Ballymoney

Motorcross Bike

When I pulled my bike
Out of the van
To have a ride
That was my plan.

I put on my helmet
And started it up
All of a sudden
It just blew up.

We tried to fix it
But it was too hard
My dad said something dreadful
'We'll take it to the scrapyard!'

Adam McFaull (10)
Kilmoyle Primary School, Ballymoney

Snowy Days

Across the fields it's quiet and still,
As the snow lies on the top of every hill.
Children rush out to play,
Though it is a snowy day.

I go to Grandpa's house to play,
For he has got a big sleigh.
Over we walk to the hill,
I can't wait, it's such a thrill.

Let it snow, let it snow,
No one wants it to go.
Being out in the snow is fun,
Some even say it is better than the sun.

Melissa Kane (10)
Kilmoyle Primary School, Ballymoney

Snow

As I look outside and see the snow,
Straight away I clearly know.
I am going to have a really fun day,
Having a snowball fight as we play.

All my friends throwing snowballs at me,
There is so much snow I can hardly see.
It is so very, very, very scary,
But the worst person of all is a boy called Terry!

As I look out and see the snow,
It is so beautiful the way it glows.
It's white and shimmering all day long,
While my friends and I make up a snow song.

Charis Nevin (9)
Kilmoyle Primary School, Ballymoney

Snow Is Falling

As I look out and see the snow,
Straight away just then I know.
I'm going to have a snowball fight,
I just hope that I don't get frostbite.

As snow is falling all around,
All I can see is white on the ground.
Icicles twinkling, what a pretty sight,
Showing beautiful colours in the bright light.

Trees are frosting all day long,
While my friends and I make up a snow song.
As the day is nearly over I'm very, very sad,
The snow I hope will stay until tomorrow so I'm actually quite glad.

Olivia Boyd (10)
Kilmoyle Primary School, Ballymoney

Me - Moving At School

I zip and zoom,
I shout and slip,
I scramble, subtract and sit.
I divide and dodge,
I laugh and leap
And frequently I spit.

I flee and flow,
I hurry and hide,
I challenge, compete and contend.
I race and rush,
I crawl and creep
And now and then I pretend!

Thomas McCrory (9)
Kilmoyle Primary School, Ballymoney

Me - Moving At School

I work and write,
I talk and trip,
I shout, slip and slide.
I dart and dash,
I dodge and draw
And frequently I divide.

I pay and play,
I leap and laugh,
I turn, tick and trap.
I walk and wash,
I fight and flick
And now and then I rap.

Craig McKeeman (10)
Kilmoyle Primary School, Ballymoney

Winter

Winter's sometimes fun
But there's lots of ice.
Sometimes it's miserable,
Sometimes it's nice.
My brothers and I like to play in the snow.
Winter's icy breath makes our cheeks glow.
It freezes my toes,
It reddens my nose,
But sliding on ice can be fun I suppose.

Joshua-James McKee (11)
Loanends Primary School, Crumlin

Old Man Winter

I hear you skiing on my roof.
I hear the ice freezing on your beard.
I see your footprint on the lawn.
There are white flakes coming from the sky.
Is it your dandruff?
I hope you are OK out there.
It is bitterly cold.
I hope I see you next year.

William Adair (11)
Loanends Primary School, Crumlin

Fear

I hate you Fear, I really do.
You always hang about me turning
My stomach until I feel sick.
You are so cold and always making things worse.
I hate you Fear, I really do.

PJ Bowman (11)
Loanends Primary School, Crumlin

Winter

Heart of ice and fingers like icicles.
Old as the ground and when the time of the year turns to you
You turn into an ice palace.
The frost twinkles on the grass and the pond is shiny as can be,
But you never want to let spring out,
You never want the leaves to grow back
And some people want flowers to burst up from the ground.
They want to see the year go by.

Joshua Walker (11)
Loanends Primary School, Crumlin

Fear

You are dark and I tremble,
Even though it's not cold,
There are eyes in the trees,
I am afraid to turn round,
There is a silence in the air,
Although a haunting sound,
I am scared and alone,
'Is anybody there?'

Sophie Martin (11)
Loanends Primary School, Crumlin

Winter

Winter, why be so blue?
With your sparkling icicles and frosty view.

You creep around like a shadow in the dark
Sprinkling snow all over the park.

When nightfall comes you slink around
Trailing snow all over the ground.

Emma McWhirter (11)
Loanends Primary School, Crumlin

The Dark, Dark Night

Walking up the peaceful path,
Don't slip, said the danger sign.
The night got darker and darker
And there was an alarming cry.
'Hush, don't be frightened,'
Said a voice in my head.
'It's only the howl of a wolf,' it said.

Edward Stirling (11)
Loanends Primary School, Crumlin

Winter

Old Man Winter bouncing from cloud to cloud, making it snow,
With his white leather boots,
With his white leather trousers and a big furry coat.
You make the roads hostile and dangerous.
Your breath makes the grass as hard as rock.
After you lay down your blanket of snow
The children come out to laugh and play.

Philip White (11)
Loanends Primary School, Crumlin

Fear

Fear is a stranger lurking in the corner,
Nearby to its brother, Death.
Hiding in your imagination,
Waiting in your nightmares.
He is like a shadow, silent but sly,
Creeping around inside your mind,
Keep away from Fear's corner.

Olivia Catherine Anna Fleming (11)
Loanends Primary School, Crumlin

Winter

Winter, winter, why do you hang around so?
I do not see the point of you being here,
When you are so lonely.
Winter, winter, you're oh so cold and hostile,
You're getting old now, please let young, little
Spring come out and play!

Rose Marquess (11)
Loanends Primary School, Crumlin

Countdown To Blast-Off!

10 . . .
Did I pack pants?
9 . . .
Why do I have to go?
8 . . .
Will I get fed there?
7 . . .
Is my heart going to explode?
6 . . .
Are there flowers in this galaxy?
5 . . .
Can I see aliens?
4 . . .
Where will I sleep?
3 . . .
Are there games?
2 . . .
Did I feed my mouse?
1 . . .
Did I go to the toilet?

Blast-off!

Emma Wallace (9)
Macosquin Primary School, Coleraine

Countdown To Blast-Off!

10 . . .
Should I go to the toilet?
9 . . .
Did I bring socks?
8 . . .
Are all the buttons working?
7 . . .
How is the journey?
6 . . .
Did I feed my pony?
5 . . .
Are there other people there?
4 . . .
Where is my food?
3 . . .
Are there shops there?
2 . . .
Do I really have to go?
1 . . .
Can we go yet?

Blast-off!

Maxine Smyth (9)
Macosquin Primary School, Coleraine

Countdown To Blast-Off!

10 . . .
Did I turn off the gas in my house?
9 . . .
Did I turn off the TV?
8 . . .
Did I feed my rabbit?
7 . . .
Did I clean my rabbit's hutch?
6 . . .
Did I give my brother his chore book?
5 . . .
Where is my extra food?
4 . . .
Did my friend come over to look after my rabbit?
3 . . .
Did I leave the keys under the mat?
2 . . .
Where did I put my oxygen tank?
1 . . .
Is there enough fuel in the capsule?

Blast-off!

Heléna Scott (9)
Macosquin Primary School, Coleraine

Countdown To Blast-Off!

10 . . .
How long is it going to take?
9 . . .
Will I be able to see the moon?
8 . . .
Will we go past the sun?
7 . . .
Will I see the stars?
6 . . .
How many days will we be there?
5 . . .
I feel really excited!
4 . . .
How long until blast-off?
3 . . .
Is it time to say goodbye?
2 . . .
The board is counting down very fast!
1 . . .
Time to go!

Blast-off!

Timothy Reid (8)
Macosquin Primary School, Coleraine

Countdown To Blast-Off!

10 . . .
Are there aliens?
9 . . .
Did I bring enough air?
8 . . .
I am scared!
7 . . .
Did I go to the toilet?
6 . . .
Do I know how to drive this rocket?
5 . . .
I feel really hungry!
4 . . .
Are people watching me from the ground?
3 . . .
Is my friend ready to go?
2 . . .
Are we nearly ready to go?
1 . . .
Here we go!

Blast-off!

Ben Ross (8)
Macosquin Primary School, Coleraine

Countdown To Blast-Off!

10 . . .
How did I get here?
9 . . .
Where am I?
8 . . .
Did I change the baby's nappy?
7 . . .
Where are the car keys?
6 . . .
What did I eat for breakfast?
5 . . .
Did I lock the car?
4 . . .
Did I change my pants?
3 . . .
Did I do my homework?
2 . . .
Did I lock the garage?
1 . . .
Did I lock the house?

Blast-off!

Kaitlin Campbell (9)
Macosquin Primary School, Coleraine

Countdown To Blast-Off!

10 . . .
I wonder what the weather is like.
9 . . .
Did I say goodbye to my friends?
8 . . .
How long will it take to get there?
7 . . .
Where is my dog?
6 . . .
Is space big?
5 . . .
I wonder if there are aliens.
4 . . .
Will I be happy there?
3 . . .
Will my dog miss me?
2 . . .
Did I feed my pet Jill?
1 . . .
Will my family miss me?

Blast-off!

Charlotte Dorrans (9)
Macosquin Primary School, Coleraine

Countdown To Blast-Off!

10 . . .
Why do people go to Mars?
9 . . .
How many people have gone to space?
8 . . .
Did I remember to feed the fish?
7 . . .
Will I miss one of the planets?
6 . . .
Did I brush my hair?
5 . . .
Is it hot or cold on the moon?
4 . . .
Are there aliens in space?
3 . . .
Will I be happy there?
2 . . .
Will I miss my little brother?
1 . . .
How will I get on?

Blast-off!

Natasha Hall (9)
Macosquin Primary School, Coleraine

Countdown To Blast-Off!

10 . . .
Why do astronauts not walk on the moon?
9 . . .
Why do astronauts go to Saturn?
8 . . .
Why don't astronauts sleep on the moon?
7 . . .
Why did God make space?
6 . . .
Is Mummy OK?
5 . . .
Why did I go?
4 . . .
Why do astronauts go to space?
3 . . .
Why do children not go?
2 . . .
Why do the astronauts not say no?
1 . . .
Why don't the astronauts go home?

Blast-off!

Marla Stewart (9)
Macosquin Primary School, Coleraine

Santa Claus

He has an ugly beard
He has boots covered in coal
He lives at the North Pole
He is as fat as a pig
He is as slow as a sloth

He is Santa Claus.

Ruairí McKillop (9)
St Columbas Primary School, Coleraine

Happy People

H appy people
A re having the time of their lives
P eople welcoming you
P eople having lots of fun
Y ou're playing lots of games

P arty lots and lots
E njoying
O n the move
P lay lots of games
L oving the time
E ating lots of food.

Dylan Mullan (10)
St Columbas Primary School, Coleraine

Jamie Entertainment

J oe McElderry is his best friend.
A jolly good singer he is.
M aroon is the colour of his hair.
I like his singing very much.
E verybody in my family likes him.

A nyone would like to be him.
R ushing to sing to the crowd.
'C ome on, rock the stage,' he says.
H is hair is like a hedge.
E ven his dancing is amazing.
R aises his voice to make the song good.

Aidan Davidson (8)
St Columbas Primary School, Coleraine

My Friend Grace

G race is a great friend to me.
R osy on her cheeks.
A thletics is her passion.
C ute as a button.
E ager to play her guitar.

M agic is not her thing.
U nderstands you when you're upset.
L ovely as a flower.
L oving as a mummy.
A vailable any time.
N imble, moves easily.

Megan McGilligan (7)
St Columbas Primary School, Coleraine

A Special Rock Star

M iley Cyrus is a rock princess
I heard she lives in Tennessee
L ike a cheetah she's fast
E verything she's in I watch
Y oghurt she eats for break

C ameras flash when she comes out
Y es she does do autographs
R abbits are her favourite animal
U mbrellas for her are sparkled with glitter
S he has a great singing voice.

Anthony Davidson (8)
St Columbas Primary School, Coleraine

Miley Cyrus

M iley has golden hair like the sun.
I think her nails are like sharp knives.
L illy is her number one fan.
E ach fan dazzles in the crowd.
Y ellow is her 3rd favourite colour.

C ream and strawberries are her favourite foods.
Y oghurt is her 2nd favourite food.
R ock music is her favourite music.
'U nderneath the Blue Sky' is her best song.
S he is as beautiful as a butterfly.

Grace Mullan (8)
St Columbas Primary School, Coleraine

Smarty Pants

As fast as Spider Pig.
As fat as the Earth.
As big as an elephant.
As wobbly as a jelly.
As stupid as a sloth.
As silly as a monkey.
As funny as a clown.
As clumsy as a roly-poly dog.
As popular as a film star.

It's Smarty Pants.

Keeley Shaye Faulkner (8)
St Columbas Primary School, Coleraine

All Aboard the Poetry Express

My Brother

Penny lover
TV hogger
Nose flicking
Clocks ticking
Out at day
He lives to play
He likes his brain
Gets on the train
Thinks he's cool
Hates his school.

Mairead Tully (10)
St Columbas Primary School, Coleraine

Beyoncé Knowles Poem!

She's as beautiful as a butterfly.
She's so energetic.
She's very cool.
She's as thin as a pencil.
She's a fabulous artist.
She's a brilliant singer.
I love her songs.

She's Beyoncé!

Caitlín Moore (7)
St Columbas Primary School, Coleraine

A Werewolf Poem

As strong as a man.
As loud as a lion.
As furry as a coat.
As dangerous as a wolf.
As fast as a cheetah.
As brave as a tiger.
As quick as a bird.
It is a werewolf.

Aoife Gallagher (8)
St Columbas Primary School, Coleraine

Cousin Ciaran

He is as fast as my roller skates.
He is as loud as a wolf.
He is as bad as a bull.
He is as big as my friend Jack.
He is as funny as a monkey.
He is as strong as a man.
He is my cousin Ciaran.

Seán McKillop (8)
St Columbas Primary School, Coleraine

Vikings

V icious Vikings
I nvading islands
K illing people
I n longships
N aughty
G reedy Gorbs
S melly.

Matthew Connolly (9)
St Columbas Primary School, Coleraine

Snow And Summer

Snow
Cold, white
Freezing, snowman, frosty
Icy, snowy, holiday, family
Shining, picnicking, sunbathing
Warm, sunny
Summer.

Tiernán O'Connell (10)
St Columbas Primary School, Coleraine

My Best Friend Jack

He's very funny, he's like a clown.
He smiles like the sun.
He's as fast as a lion.
He's as happy as a monkey.
He's as smart as a kangaroo.
He's as silly as a dog.
He's my best friend Jack.

Killian Mullan (9)
St Columbas Primary School, Coleraine

Friends

F riends forever
R eally kind
I ntelligent always, never-
E nding friendship
N ever-ending fun
D o not grow apart
S o they just have fun.

Kathleen Cassidy (9)
St Columbas Primary School, Coleraine

Cheeky Chimps

Cheeky monkeys chattering to each other.
Eating bananas all day long.
Swinging and jumping, running and chasing.
These cheeky little chimps have fun all day.
People come to watch them put on a show!
Monkeys, monkeys, running to and fro!

Shauna Deighan (9)
St Columbas Primary School, Coleraine

My Friend Killian

He is as small as an elephant.
He is as funny as a monkey.
He is brighter than the sun.
He is as good as Ronaldo.
He is good fun.
He is my friend Killian.

Jack Robinson (9)
St Columbas Primary School, Coleraine

School

S chool is fun.
C lapping when someone's won.
H appy at school with my friends.
O utside at break time.
O utside after lunchtime.
L ucky to be at school.

Nadine O'Kane (9)
St Columbas Primary School, Coleraine

Newborn

Soft skin
Blue eyes
Small nose
Big smile
Teardrops running down each cheek
Make her have a happy life.

Hannah Mullan (9)
St Columbas Primary School, Coleraine

Ninja Cat

It is daring
It is fearless
It will fight off any dog
It will even eat chilli
It is as fast as lightning
It sleeps all day and hunts all night

It is my cat Nixo.

Nathan James Totten (7)
St MacNissius Primary School, Tannaghmore

Mystery Guest Riddle

She is as beautiful as a peacock.
She is a judge in a programme.
She is as bright as the sun.
She wears fashionable clothes.
She is as friendly as a dog.
She is Dannii Minogue.

Kimberley McCallum (7)
St MacNissius Primary School, Tannaghmore

Mystery Guest Riddle

It is as hairy as a bear.
It eats bananas.
It is really ugly.
It is huge.
It is scary.
It is King Kong.

Tara Heffron (8)
St MacNissius Primary School, Tannaghmore

Daydreams

Mr Fleming thinks I'm reading
But I'm dancing in a show,
Or being a monkey . . .
I'm up in the air . . .
Or flying around the world.
I have a fight with my friend
And my cousin . . .
I go home at ten with a busted nose
My cousin gave me.

Mr Fleming thinks I'm listening -
But no,
I'm at a wrestling match . . .
I'm diving into water,
Or throwing balls at the wall.
I'm a strong woman big and bad . . .
I jump and float in a big hot tub,
Lying in the clouds, lying gently.

I think of putting on a show in a big sports car.
The wind rushing by as I walk round the bend
And I jump in a duck pond.
When I wake up I am bad-tempered because I'm tired.

Amy Whoriskey (10)
St Paul's Primary School, Galliagh

Daydreams

Mr Fleming thinks I'm reading
But I'm at the zoo with the monkeys
Or doing laps in a marathon
I'm out fishing with my cousins
I'm out swimming with my friends
I go to the driving range for an hour
I go to Spain for a month
I'm at a Liverpool match.

Mr Fleming thinks I am listening
But no
I'm fighting for my kickboxing team
I get a new dog for my birthday
I've won a million pounds in the lotto
I'm a famous actor
I own an estate with a 1,000 houses
I've gone to Hollywood to live
I own two Ferraris and seven jeeps!

I think of winning a Ferrari race
I score the winning goal for Liverpool in the Cup Final
I find a dead person in a desert
When I wake up I have one sum done
Mr Fleming isn't happy!

Sean Damien Reid (11)
St Paul's Primary School, Galliagh

Daydreams

Mr Fleming thinks I'm reading but no
I'm thinking of what we will be doing for PE
I think I am driving a Lamborghini
I am getting out and the doors are going up sidewards
I am scoring the winning goal in the FA Cup Final
I am flying really high in a hot air balloon
I've won the Lotto and get £7,000,000!

Mr Fleming thinks I'm listening but no
I am fighting crocodiles
I'm jumping off Mount Everest
I have found the Titanic and get millions
I am the second man on the moon
I am bungee-jumping off the moon
I have kicked all of the shark's teeth down his throat!

I am the world's best footballer
I am the one who knocked down the Twin Towers
I'm boxing John Duddy
I'm the world's greatest engineer
I think Mr Fleming's staring at me saying, 'What are you doing?'
Wait a minute, he actually is!

Michael Anthony Lindsay (11)
St Paul's Primary School, Galliagh

Football

I really, really like football,
I play it all the time,
The referee gave a bad call today,
But I just thought it was a crime.

I really, really like Arsenal,
I watch them play all the time,
Today I got a letter from the council,
They said there has been a crime.

My favourite player is Walcott,
Last week he had a bad fall,
He always scores a lot,
Even though he is very small.

He is really, really fast,
He runs up the line like a shot,
Today he ran past all of the defenders
And he wasn't even caught!

Today at football,
I scored a good header,
Too bad it couldn't be better!

Bradley Belgrave (10)
St Paul's Primary School, Galliagh

Hot Chocolate

It's 3 o'clock and it's raining heavily.
I see children rushing home through the grass and getting covered in muck.
I feel like I just had a swim in the swimming pool!
A woman with a giant umbrella is running quickly to catch the bus.
A dog runs to get shelter, he looks frightened.
I hear cars splashing in a big giant puddle and soaking a small, cold child.
I see little children with yellow wellies on splashing in puddles.
I see a black and white cat running under a car
And it hides under the wheel of the car.
I see a boy running in the puddles, he might get grounded.
I hear a man on the phone and he is saying, 'Can I get a taxi, please?'
I hear rain on my head going *pit-pat, pit-pat!*
I see a person getting in a car and I say to myself, 'I wish I was her.'
I get home, I see a warm hot chocolate and a cookie sitting on the table.
My mum gets me a warm towel and a teddy bear.
I am happy.

Ciara O'Doherty (10)
St Paul's Primary School, Galliagh

Hot Stew

3 o'clock and I'm getting ready to go home.
Heavy rain falling from the sky.
Christine and I are dripping wet.
Rain bouncing on the puddles making circles.
My jeans sticking to my legs.
I'm so cold.
A nice warm bowl of stew with red sauce.
When I get home I put on my PJs and snuggle up to my mum.

Shanice Boyle (10)
St Paul's Primary School, Galliagh

Springtime

The sun is shining,
The birds are singing,
The sky is so blue,
The joy is all around.

The children are laughing,
My dad is golfing,
It is springtime again,
It's that which makes me happy.

Animals are waking from their winter sleep,
The cold is away,
The warmth has arrived.

The grass is so green,
The flowers are growing,
It's a wonderful time of the year.

Christopher McQuaid (10)
St Paul's Primary School, Galliagh

I Saw A Peacock . . .

I saw a peacock stand on his head
I saw a boy bark at the postman
I saw a dog fit a floor
I saw a baby fly a plane
I saw a pilot chase a cat
I saw a dog play on the PSP
I saw a girl in her kennel
I saw a dog reading two books
I saw a teacher in his hutch
I saw a rabbit walk down the street
I saw a man in his hole
I saw a mouse in the mist of night
I saw the child who saw these wondrous things.

Jack Gillen (10)
St Paul's Primary School, Galliagh

My Dog Boots

My dog, Boots, is cute and funny,
She loves the fog but she hates the bog,
Once she ate a frog!
My dog, Boots, hurt her paw
And it was raw.
She likes to run and fall,
She used to be small but now she is tall.
My dog, Boots, is the best,
She wore a vest but she has a hairy chest!
She ate a doll,
She played with her ball.
She is the best in the world
Because she is my tiger baby
And she is only one year old.

Aoife Robinson (10)
St Paul's Primary School, Galliagh

Life

Life is good
Life is great
It is like the number eight

It goes round
Round and round
Nearly like a merry-go-round

Life is fun
Like a run
Through the grass

Then you realise
You're in class.

Caitlin Goodfellow (10)
St Paul's Primary School, Galliagh

I Saw A Peacock . . .

I saw a peacock drive a car,
I saw a man swallow a girl whole,
I saw a python read a book,
I saw a librarian do a backflip,
I saw a gymnast eat a zebra,
I saw a crocodile make my homework,
I saw Mr Fleming fixing a roof,
I saw a builder play football,
I saw Connor collect nectar,
I saw a bee go to the rice bowl,
I saw a boy even in the midst of the night,
I saw a child that saw a wondrous sight.

Reece Ogle (11)
St Paul's Primary School, Galliagh

Summertime

Summer days are long and bright
I like to always play till night.
My friends and I like to have fun
Because we have so much fun with everyone.
There are lots of things we can do
Like go to the beach and have a barbecue.
There are lots of people all about,
I get my ball and kick about.
Summertime is lots of fun,
It means a lot to everyone.

Rhys Dunne (10)
St Paul's Primary School, Galliagh

My Dog Lucky

I've got a dog, his name is Lucky.
Sometimes he comes in from the street looking rather mucky.
Mum puts him in the bath and this makes me really laugh
When I see his face all wet and huffy.
Later he sits in his bed
And scratches his head
And I think, *oh what a bad puppy.*
I give him a treat and he eats from the street
And I think, *oh what would I do without my Lucky?*

Inaam Abdallah (10)
St Paul's Primary School, Galliagh

Spring Is Coming

Spring is my favourite time of the year
I love it when the flowers begin to bloom
Their bright colours shine in the warm sunshine
Oh spring is my favourite time of year.

The nights are getting lighter
The clocks are soon to change
We can all stay in the park much longer
Hip, hip, hip, hip, hooray.

Reece Moore (10)
St Paul's Primary School, Galliagh

Who Is De Girl?

Who is de girl dat likes to laugh
And went home for de bath?

Rebecca is de girl so full o zest
Rebecca is de girl dat just can't rest.

Who is de girl dat fell
Den went for water in de well?

Rebecca is de girl so full o zest
Rebecca is de girl dat just can't rest.

Who is de girl dat was small
And learned how to crawl?

Rebecca is de girl so full o zest
Rebecca is de girl dat just can't rest.

Who is de girl dat likes to play
But fell into hay?

Rebecca is de girl so full o zest
Rebecca is de girl dat just can't rest.

Who is de girl dat ran in a race
But went to some random place?

Rebecca is de girl so full o zest
Rebecca is de girl dat just can't rest.

Who is de girl dat sat on a rock
And went home when her clock went tick-tock?

Rebecca is de girl so full o zest
Rebecca is de girl dat just can't rest.

Rebecca McDermott (10)
Sacred Heart Primary School, Waterside

Who Is De Girl?

Who is de girl dat likes to have fun
Den she is playing in de sun?

Niamh is a girl so full o zest
Niamh is a girl dat just can't rest.

Who is de girl dat never came to school
But only because she acted like a fool?

Niamh is a girl so full o zest
Niamh is a girl dat just can't rest.

Who is de girl dat likes to sing
And never hears the telephone ring?

Niamh is a girl so full o zest
Niamh is a girl dat just can't rest.

Who is de girl dat has a cat
And doesn't play baseball with a bat?

Niamh is a girl so full o zest
Niamh is a girl dat just can't rest.

Who is de girl dat sits at home
And decided to use her comb?

Niamh is a girl so full o zest
Niamh is a girl dat just can't rest.

Who is de girl dat likes to jump
And rides on a camel with a big hump?

Niamh is a girl so full o zest
Niamh is a girl dat just can't rest.

Niamh Kelly (10)
Sacred Heart Primary School, Waterside

Chinese Sandman

Chinese sandmen wise and creepy,
Croon dream songs to make us sleepy.

Fireflies glow and gleam,
But their hidden bite is so mean.

Chinese sandmen wise and creepy,
Croon dream songs to make us sleepy.

Be careful you don't fall asleep,
Or he'll jump at you with a giant leap.

Chinese sandmen wise and creepy,
Croon dream songs to make us sleepy.

Swallows are such peaceful birds,
But did you notice they don't say any words?

Chinese sandmen wise and creepy,
Croon dream songs to make us sleepy.

Owls come out at night,
Then fall asleep at the crack of light.

Chinese sandmen wise and creepy,
Croon dream songs to make us sleepy.

Rivers rage down the hill,
And power the large windmill.

Chinese sandmen wise and creepy,
Croon dream songs to make us sleepy.

Boars run around the bank,
Before the sky turns pitch-black.

Ben McLaughlin (10)
Sacred Heart Primary School, Waterside

Who Is De Boy?

Who is de boy dat made dat park?
Who is de boy dat done a fart?

Ben is de boy so full o zest
Ben is de boy dat just can't rest.

Who is de boy dat is so funny?
Who is de boy who bought a bunny?

Ben is de boy so full o zest
Ben is de boy dat just can't rest.

Who is de boy dat hates school?
Who is de boy dat jumps in da pool?

Ben is de boy so full o zest
Ben is de boy dat just can't rest.

Who is de boy dat is so smart?
Who is de boy dat works in da kwik-e-mart?

Ben is de boy so full o zest
Ben is de boy dat just can't rest.

Who is de boy dat loves her?
Who is de boy dat is poor?

Ben is de boy so full o zest
Ben is de boy dat just can't rest.

Ben Radcliff (9)
Sacred Heart Primary School, Waterside

All Aboard the Poetry Express

Untitled

Shannon is de girl so full o zest
Shannon is de girl dat just can't rest.

Who is de girl dat wears skinny jeans
But has time to eat beans?

Shannon is de girl so full o zest
Shannon is de girl dat just can't rest.

Who is de girl dat has money
Then bought a bunny?

Shannon is de girl so full o zest
Shannon is de girl dat just can't rest.

Who is de girl dat says bye
Then throws her dog up to the sky?

Shannon is de girl so full o zest
Shannon is de girl dat just can't rest.

Who is de girl dat colours in
Den drow it in de bin?

Shannon is de girl so full o zest
Shannon is de girl dat just can't rest.

Shannon McConomy (9)
Sacred Heart Primary School, Waterside

Teacher, Teacher

Teacher, teacher come here quick,
I have got better at a football trick.

Teacher, teacher I've gone mad,
At that boy that's always bad.

Teacher, teacher give me my stool,
So I can work with my tools.

Teacher, teacher come and look,
Aoifen is a big fat cook.

Teacher, teacher he stole my trolley,
Ben is such a big fat bully.

Teacher, teacher in my hand,
Everybody loves Peter Pan.

Teacher, teacher Aoifen's so smelly
And his belly is really hairy.

Teacher, teacher sheep's so woolly,
Do you know my sister Molly?

Teacher, teacher I see a rat,
Go and hide behind that mat.

Aoifen McBrearty (10)
Sacred Heart Primary School, Waterside

Who Is De Boy?

Who is de boy dat got a scare
Den went home and said a prayer?

Cahir is a boy so full o jest
Cahir is a boy dat just can't rest.

Who is de boy who had a pear?
From over here it has a hair.

Cahir is a boy so full o jest
Cahir is a boy dat just can't rest.

Who is de boy dat cried
'Cause he didn't get a piece of pie?

Cahir is a boy so full o zest
Cahir is a boy dat just can't rest.

Who is the boy dat got off the plane?
Then someone called him a name.

Cahir is a boy so full o zest
Cahir is a boy dat just can't rest.

Cahir Henderson (9)
Sacred Heart Primary School, Waterside

Who Is De Girl?

Who is de girl dat played with a dog
And den ran home in the fog?

Aoife is de girl full o zest
Aoife is de girl dat just can't rest.

Who is de girl dat went to school
And at de end of de day made a new rule?

Aoife is de girl full o zest
Aoife is de girl dat just can't rest.

Who is de girl dat went for a swim
And den ate some cheese dat tasted quite grim?

Aoife is de girl full o zest
Aoife is de girl dat just can't rest.

Who is de girl dat climbed up de tree
And at the top it was hard to see?

Aoife is de girl full o zest
Aoife is de girl dat just can't rest.

Aoife Strawbridge (10)
Sacred Heart Primary School, Waterside

Who Is De Girl?

Who is de girl dat brushes her hair
Den rips her shoe with a big tear?

Sarah is de girl dat just can't rest
Sarah is de girl so full o zest.

Who is de girl dat swims ten miles
Den swishes off to the sky and flies?

Sarah is de girl so full o zest
Sarah is de girl dat just can't rest.

Who is de girl dat falls off de tree
Den with a bang hurts her knee?

Sarah is de girl so full o zest
Sarah is de girl dat just can't rest.

Who is de girl dat pushes the cart
Then starts to eat some jam tarts?

Sarah Owens (9)
Sacred Heart Primary School, Waterside

Teacher, Teacher

Teacher, teacher it is time,
To go and see the funny mime!

Teacher, teacher I prefer,
To have a day at the fair!

Teacher, teacher in the kart,
Someone has just won a tart!

Teacher, teacher will you look at that?
There's a big, fluffy dog on our mat.

Teacher, teacher Caelan's best,
Because he's so full of zest!

Alisha Villa (10)
Sacred Heart Primary School, Waterside

Who Is De Boy?

Who is de boy dat ate a tart
Den sat on a red dart?

Adam is a boy so full o zest
Adam is a boy dat just can't rest.

Who is de boy dat plays de Xbox
And stays home with chickenpox?

Adam is a boy so full o zest
Adam is a boy dat just can't rest.

Who is de boy dat climbed the tree?
De ball was lost, he couldn't see.

Adam is a boy so full o zest
Adam is a boy dat just can't rest.

Who is de boy dat fell on de ground
Den sent his dog back to the pound?

Adam McGlinchey (10)
Sacred Heart Primary School, Waterside

Teacher, Teacher

Teacher, teacher come and look
Seamus is getting eaten by a book

Teacher, teacher you are so smelly
And you have a big fat belly

Teacher, teacher I have gone mad
Look at that boy he is so bad

Teacher, teacher you are so thin
You could fit inside a bin

Teacher, teacher you are a rat
Please hit Adam with a baseball bat.

Caoimhín Ballard (10)
Sacred Heart Primary School, Waterside

Teacher, Teacher

Teacher, teacher it's 3 o'clock
And I've lost my football sock

Teacher, teacher *look* over there
That man has funny hair

Teacher, teacher you are mad
Because I was really bad

Teacher, teacher it is 5 to 3
Please give me my cheese

Teacher, teacher please be fair
And give me my friend's underwear

Teacher, teacher don't be dumb
Go and suck your thumb

Teacher, teacher I'm so lame
I hurt myself on the climbing frame.

Gemma Boyle (9)
Sacred Heart Primary School, Waterside

Teacher, Teacher

Teacher, teacher go and see
Great big bumblebee.
Teacher, teacher I'm so cool
Get me out of this school.
Teacher, teacher you're so cool,
Take us to the swimming pool.
Teacher, teacher have a look
The silly boy hurt the cook.
Teacher, teacher go and see
The billy goat have a cup of tea.

Georgia Hildreth (9)
Sacred Heart Primary School, Waterside

Chinese New Year

C elebration for Chinese people
H appiness and joy all around
I maginations open
N ever let it end
E very year it's a different date
S weeping and cleaning everywhere
E njoy it while it lasts

N ever forgetting this day
E verybody gets together
W herever you go in China you will see joy

Y oung children get money or sweets
E xciting
A lot of colour, bright everywhere
R emembering relatives.

Ren Thompson (8)
Tonagh Primary School, Lisburn

Walking

A tight street
Some sore feet
Some torn shoes
Some wet trousers
Some numb feet
One sore foot
Some awful bags
Keeps you down
Drags you about
Makes you tired
You fall down.

Claire Smylie (10)
Tonagh Primary School, Lisburn

Blimp

A hydrogen eater
An air exploder
A giant flyer
An oxygen blower
A strange diver
A propeller user
A passenger carrier
A cloud transporter
A colossal drifter
A balloon masterpiece.

Lucas Jack Fitzsimmons (10)
Tonagh Primary School, Lisburn

Bus

A big red
A steamy engine
A traffic pusher
A double-decker
A bouncy maniac
A big glow
A comfy seat
A people carrier
A grinding mover
A bumper car.

Nathan Brennan (9)
Tonagh Primary School, Lisburn

Lorry

A hard turner
A loud beeper
A road blocker
A goods carrier
A tyre screecher
A road blocker
An every day traveller
A heavy loader
A box holder
A road user.

Skye McMichael (10)
Tonagh Primary School, Lisburn

Winter

Winter feels cold
Winter looks like ice cream
Winter tastes freezing
Winter smells fresh
Winter sounds like laughter.

Dean McCann (8)
Tonagh Primary School, Lisburn

Winter

Winter feels like a warm bed
Winter looks like a big blanket
Winter tastes like hot chocolate
Winter smells like hot buns
Winter sounds like rain hitting off the window.

Ben Lancaster (8)
Tonagh Primary School, Lisburn

Winter

Winter feels cold outside.
Winter looks like real fun.
Winter tastes like water.
Winter smells fresh.
Winter sounds nice.

Ethan Louden (8)
Tonagh Primary School, Lisburn

Winter

Winter feels cold
Winter looks snowy
Winter tastes icy
Winter smells like ice cream
Winter sounds quiet.

Sarah O'Flaherty (8)
Tonagh Primary School, Lisburn

Winter

Winter looks snowy and beautiful
Winter feels frosty and cold
Winter tastes like freshly bought milk
Winter sounds like wind blowing against my window
Winter smells like ice on the top of my nose.

Katie Chesney (7)
Tonagh Primary School, Lisburn

Winter

Winter feels like warm fire.
Winter looks like a white blanket.
Winter tastes like water.
Winter smells great.
Winter sounds like wind blowing against the window.

Joshua Robertson (8)
Tonagh Primary School, Lisburn

Winter

Winter feels cold
Winter looks like ice cream
Winter tastes freezing
Winter smells fresh
Winter sounds noisy.

Scott McBride
Tonagh Primary School, Lisburn

Snow

S now is soft
N ice and white
O ut of the sky
W onderful and bright.

Skye Elizabeth Dodd (8)
Tonagh Primary School, Lisburn

Young Writers Information

We hope you have enjoyed reading this book - and that you will continue to enjoy it in the coming years.

If you like reading and writing poetry drop us a line, or give us a call, and we'll send you a free information pack.

Alternatively if you would like to order further copies of this book or any of our other titles, then please give us a call or log onto our website at **www.youngwriters.co.uk**.

Young Writers Information
Remus House
Coltsfoot Drive
Peterborough
PE2 9JX
(01733) 890066

A platform for your poetry!

Get in touch!